To Diana,

MW00354602

Jump & The Joy Will Follow
How to Live in Conscious Joy and Health in Every Stage of Life.

May we jump together and for joy, make a difference in the world,

Linda

Printed in the United States of America.

Library of Congress Control Number: 2006910477

ISBN 1-4196-3787-8

10 9 8 7 6 5 4 3 2 1

First Paperback Edition

Cover and interior design by Riggs Creative Group
www.riggscreative.com

Dedication

I dedicate the words in this book to Vannessa, Vivianne, and Jennifer, and to all the daughters who were sent from above to teach their mothers to be stronger, wiser, and happier.

My three daughters have always been my raison d'etre, my pride, my justification for being on earth. I have been the most blessed of women because these three such different, powerful, and unique women have shared my life.

It wasn't because I expected them to be such exceptional women; it wasn't because I knew that when they grew up they would be my counselors, my supporters, my stabilizers; it wasn't even because I was perceptive enough to futurize that each of them, in their own way, would be shining stars in their professions. They were my inspirations, just because the universe put us together.

We made each other special. We fed on each other's unique differences. I remember strangers, after observing us playing and laughing in the park or at the beach, commenting on our shared joy. I would thank them, look at them teary eyed, and say, "It's because we chose each other."

Having only girls in a macho world could have paralyzed us, but it just made us stronger, closer, prouder, smarter, and relentlessly supportive of each other. Our womanhood became a badge of survival and proof that women did not come unto the earth to suffer ... but to contribute, to make the planet a better place, and to love each other.

Each of us has a story to tell. And it is in the sharing and listening we discover not only how much we have in common, but the possibility to learn and maybe, even to heal each other. I invite you to tell your loved ones your story and in return to listen to theirs.

Contents

Introduction

We all know that getting older is inevitable, as we are aware that we are mortal. Yet, each of us has a different definition and image of what our personal aging process and demise looks like. This model that we hold in our heads and hearts is formed by the messages that we received from our cultures, our families, our experiences, and even evolution, and in turn, will effect how we chose to live our last years.

Some of us merely accept aging gracefully as part of life; others begrudgingly fight its symptoms to the last breath; others proudly wear the years and wrinkles like badges of honor; while still others may deny and even fear it, experiencing aging as the symbol of losing desirability and our imminent demise.

But I believe there are universal desires and needs that transcend our different views on getting older, and bind us as we enter the third stage of our lives.

We all want to wake up in the morning with meaning, connection, and love in our hearts and our lives, with enough energy to do what we want or need to do, and without physical or emotional pain. These goals are achievable, if we are willing to do the work. We don't have to get the so-called degenerative diseases of the aging, such as osteoporosis, heart failure, diabetes, or arteriosclerosis. It is scientifically proven that these diseases are preventable; they are more often symptoms of poor life style choices than genetics, or the passing of the years.

The secret to experiencing every stage of life in health and joy, is being able to answer three questions that make up life's triangle.

The What? Why? How? Triangle

Have you ever wanted to do or be something very much but haven't achieved it? For most of us the answer is yes. Whenever we find that emotionally and/or intellectually we want to achieve something in our lives, yet are unable to do so, it is because we cannot answer with conviction any or all of life's three most important questions. Why? What? How?

The WHAT requires focus and clarity. The HOW includes techniques, expertise, study, practice, consulting experts, reading. The WHY requires a willingness to do whatever it takes to go beyond perceived limitations.

If one aspect of the triangle is lacking, we will not do the work necessary to make the change and achieve the lives that we want and deserve.

For example, we want to be good parents. But, WHAT does that look like? WHAT does that mean? Maybe we are not clear. We might just know that we don't want to be like our parents. Or, we know perfectly what being a good parent entails but we don't know HOW to listen, or be patient, or be empathic, or set boundaries. Or, perhaps we are clear about what being a good parent is and how to go about it, but just don't have enough time or willingness to sacrifice what is needed to reach our goals. At this point, a strong WHY is missing.

It takes a lot of honest introspection, consciousness, and humility to realize which of the three parts of the triangle are missing. But once we do, then we know where to spend our effort and time.

By sharing with you letters to my daughters, who are my personal "why" as the backdrop to my book, I offer you the why's, what's and how's of what, in my opinion, are the nine most important elements to achieve joy and health in every stage of life. I'm sure you will come up with your own list, with its own why's, what's, and how's, and I would love to hear about them, so I can continue to benefit from, and share, the wisdom that all of us possess.

Here's to a life of health and joy, until we take our last breath! We can achieve it. I truly believe we can!

Linda's Leap Birthdays

Age 15	Age 60
February 29, 1960	February 29, 2004

From self conscious youth to unexpected joy, hope and renewal

I wrote _Jump and The Joy Will Follow_ between 2004 and 2006. Most of the letters to my daughters are dated in these two years. I have also used some letters from the 1980's and 1990's, when I divorced my husband and moved from Mexico back to the United States.

I reminisce in these letters about our lives. Some of the events I describe in the beginning of the book actually occurred after events I describe toward the end. I hope by using dates you will be able to navigate through the story, which is, after all, no more complicated than a childhood, marriage, divorce and new life after forty.

In the letters, I often reflect back to my daughters the occasions we both shared. I do this because I find it means so much to them to hear from their mother how she perceived them.

Birth: February 29, 1944

(Los Angeles, California)

Marriage: February 3, 1967

Births of daughters:

Jenny: January 20, 1968

Vivianne: July 2, 1971

Vannessa: February 15, 1974

Birth of granddaughters:

Estefania: June 29, 2001

Valentina: April 8, 2003

Divorce: 1992

Diagnosis: October, 2000

(with Grave's Disease)

Daughters' weddings:

Jenny: April 27, 1997

Vannessa: March 20, 2003

Vivianne: July 9, 2005

Sale of House: December, 2005

(in La Jolla)

"Beauty is unbearable, drives us to despair,
offering us for a minute the glimpse of an eternity
that we should like to stretch out
over the whole of time. "

~ Albert Camus

Chapter One

Beauty

(2004)

Dear Vannessa, Vivianne and Jenny,

My three beautiful daughters, thank you for wanting me to write down what you refer to as my beauty secrets. Thank you for seeing me as someone you would like to look and be like when you are my age. I look at you and am flattered and humbled, knowing that it is I who have learned so much from you about the real beauty of spirit and courage.

I hope that your motivation to remain beautiful emanates from a place of inner knowing and strength, and not from the need to please or elicit approval from others. The former, stems from a desire to glow, to shine, to be at peace in one's own skin, and puts us in control of our destiny; the latter takes away our power, and puts us at the mercy of others and their opinions.

I would like to believe that every time you look into my eyes and see my unconditional love reflecting back, you feel lovable, and as a result, beautiful. But, realistically, I know my eyes aren't the only ones that will gaze on you, and it's hard to feel desirable when the cosmetic and fashion industries spend billions of dollars perpetuating the myth we must be a size four, and under thirty in order to be considered beautiful.

I have given a lot of thought to the possibilities, challenges, and choices of combining beauty and age. I will share with you the information about the exercises I do, the creams and oils I put on my face, the supplements I take, and the organic, fresh food that I eat—even the thoughts I choose—in my effort to remain healthy, joyful and energetic ... in other words, beautiful. (I will also refer you to my web site, where I outline the latest in cosmetic procedures, though they may be obsolete by the time you might consider them.)

Here in Puerto Morelos, accompanied only by the sound of the ocean, and with no distractions from a television or the Internet, my unconscious has not let me alone. It was here, next to the ocean, that my process of introspection and brutal honesty began, and now I am able to tell the story that I never told you before. Although I have denied it, although I never wanted to admit it, although I was ashamed of it, beauty has been a very important part of my raison d'être.

However, the more time I spent investigating for you, the miraculous new options that promise to keep us physically beautiful forever, the more my unconscious hounded me. Now, at last, I understand, and I have begun to forgive myself.

I was a beautiful baby, meaning I had big, blue eyes framed by curly blonde hair, a tiny nose, and a heart-shaped mouth. My father, your Daddy-O (the nickname you gave him) was a handsome man: tall and thin, with symmetrical features and slick, black hair.

My mother was unattractive. She didn't know until later in life that she was born with a congenital disease called acromeglia, (also known as Abraham Lincoln's disease): a slow-growing tumor on the pituitary that causes the contour of the face and extremities to grow out of proportion with the rest of the body. This family triangle of the beautiful, the handsome, and the ugly, was the perfect, cruel setup for a Greek tragedy, but in our case, it was a Jewish one, which made it more complicated, and guilt ridden.

If my father had loved my mother, if he had been a deep man who saw beyond the exterior, or a moral man with intrinsic, self-imposed limitations, the tragedy could have been avoided. But he was neglected and abused as a child, and unconditional love, depth of soul, and kindness were never bestowed on him by his parents, and as a result, those loving characteristics weren't in his emotional repertoire.

In his own words, he admitted he never loved my mother, and only married her because he was going off to war and wanted to have someone waiting for his return.

Before I continue, I need to ask that you take the following into consideration. The last thing I want to do is damage, or skew, the image you have of my father, your Daddy-O. We are all wounded, all imperfect, all good and bad ... all doing the best we can in order to survive. Your Daddy-O truly loved me, as he truly loved you. He would fly thousands of miles just to attend your ballet recitals, or arrive early to be in the front seat of your graduations, or pay overweight at the airport because his luggage was filled with delightful presents and American clothes for you.

When my father returned from World War II, not only was his faithful, adoring wife awaiting him, but also a darling, little baby girl. However, what could have been a perfect postwar reunion and family was doomed from the beginning. My father, consumed with the importance of physical beauty, began to pay more attention to me than to my mom. Giving me the time and place that should have been reserved for his wife was psychologically harmful to me and painful to my mother. Believe it or not, many mothers and fathers look to their children for comfort and support instead of to their spouses, causing resentment and jealousy. This situation is more common than most people are aware of, and is called emotional incest.

My prettiness was always the center of conversation, even after my equally darling, little brother, Richie, was born. Moreover, I looked like a shiksala because of my blonde hair and blue eyes, and my shena la punim couldn't have come from my mother. I must have been adopted, onlookers would say in jest! Those undeniably cruel comments had to have been terribly painful to my mother.

As I grew up, my father took increasing pride in my looks, and I remember hearing my mother repeat unconvincingly,

"A mother always wants her progeny to be prettier than herself." This automatic, scripted reply that she must have heard a long time ago, probably kept her sane. It's hard for anyone to comprehend that we can love someone and hate them at the same time, but for my mother, this inevitable dissonance would have been impossible to accept, for a Jewish mother should love her children above all else, and all others, if not, she is not considered a good mother.

My father and I would have dinner dates before I became a teenager; alone time for father and daughter. These dinners would have been a healthy time to get to know each other, if, in reality, he hadn't been using me as a pawn to attract and conquer women. Later, when I realized that I was an unwilling accomplice to his infidelity, I felt like a traitor to my mom, who every day was becoming more hostile towards me. However, I knew if I said anything to her about those gushy, nice-smelling ladies who came to the table to admire me, I would have lost my father's love and admiration. And above all things, I wanted to safeguard his adoration.

When I was seventeen, my parents divorced. We went to court, and my brother and I had to testify. I was required to take sides and speak about the things I am now telling you. My poor mother had to endure hearing about how, not only my father, but I, had betrayed her.

So, as you see, beauty to me was a two-edged sword. I used it to ensure my father's attention, and at the same time, I was ashamed of it. Thanks to it, my daddy paid attention to me, but because of it, my mom shunned me. And because I was put in the position of having to tell the truth or lose my father's love, I was never sure if I deserved to be loved for anything else other than my appearance.

Does this shock or surprise you?

I learned very early, that in order to be loved and approved, I not only had to be pretty, I also had to be good. To be good meant always being obedient when I was a child; not standing out too brightly when I was an adolescent; not letting the boys know I was smart when I was a young woman; and not taking the initiative, or having controversial opinions when I was a wife. My best defense was to be humble, act insecure, and play down my looks. "Who me? I'm so short, and look at the bump on my nose, or how thin my hair is, and how I get freckles in the sun?"

I want you to know this is not about blame or judgment, but an attempt at self-understanding, and compassion for our frailties. By telling you this today, it is my way of

transcending and overcoming the myths and insecurities
I endured as a child. You have taught me, through your
unconditional love for me, that beauty and accomplishment
can coexist, and I can wear both my intelligence and
attractiveness proudly and confidently.

I hope it is true that as we age, we become wiser. I have
learned that holding on to negative thoughts and blame
can't be hidden from our faces. No matter how many anti-
aging crèmes or firming masks we use on the surface of our
faces, our inner lives will shine through our eyes, and we
will be able to hide our true selves less and less. We, all of
us, eventually get the face that we deserve.

My father was insecure because his own father never
acknowledged him, and his parents played one child against
the other and made them compete for their love. My mother
had to compete for the attention I got, which was rightfully
hers. No one went to therapy in those days, so the best
they could do was the best they could do. In my mother's
case, she used her favorite defense mechanism, denial, which
eventually led to resentment and anger towards me.

The anger was there when she became gravely ill and was
told by her doctor I was going to accompany her in the
ambulance to the hospital. Her loud protests made it
painfully clear that she didn't want me by her side. Yet,

once sedated, and perhaps because she no longer had a need to protect herself from the pain of ambivalence, and in a voice that was barely more than a whisper, she repeated over and over, "Linda, I'm sorry. I'm sorry. I'm sorry." The most heartbreaking part for me, was that as she took her last breath, I was unable to discern if she could hear my constant reassurance before she died. "It wasn't your fault mommy ... nothing to be sorry for ... there is nothing to forgive. I love you"

I remember thinking, "Mommy, I truly know that you loved me, and I understand why you acted the way you did. From now on, I will be your voice. I will take the risks, and dare to do everything you couldn't."

It's probably hard for you to understand what it was like growing up in a world where your talent, your intelligence, and your heart are not seen or acknowledged by others, but least of all and worst of all, not honored by yourself. In that world, my world, I wasted years of my life, fearing the loss of youth and beauty. After all, the time and money I have spent trying to maintain my looks never brought me the happiness I craved ... because Daddy never really saw me anyhow.

Writing now about physical beauty's significance in my life has begun to free me of its stranglehold. The more I think about it, and learn about its origins, the less

important it becomes. The more I go inside and see myself
... and like what I see ... the less I demand to be seen by
others. With every decision I make on my own, with
every mistake I handle well, I realize my power and
attractiveness actually have increased.

I know, I have my moments—when I feel lonely and retreat
to being that little girl seeking my daddy's approval—but each
day I take another step ... sometimes a baby step ... forward.
You must admit I've come a long way from being that
"good" girl, afraid to express myself for fear of rejection.

Vannessa, Vivianne and Jenny, my brave and beautiful
daughters, you have proven that beauty and achievement
can be combined, and when they are, the result
looks like you. Believe in yourselves, trust
your visions, and you will see that
anything is possible if you truly
believe that you deserve it.

One thing is for sure, we will
all be beautiful because we will
always be connected in love, and
this continuous, never-ending love
we share will be our gift of beauty to
our children, and to the world.

Here, my darlings, here are the secrets. (You must be thinking, "finally") Those above that come from my childhood, and those below that are ways to stay lovely to the mirror.

With beautiful thoughts and great love,

su mami

The What and How of Beauty

Appearance is the most public part of ourselves. And, having an attractive appearance seems to bestow upon its owner all sorts of positive and almost magical qualities. We expect attractive people to be better at everything; happier and healthier than most, more adroit lovers, happier spouses, richer and more successful at what ever they do. Just about every possible positive quality you can imagine is attributed to a person who is beautiful.

Although the results are unfair and outrageous, in study after study, beautiful women (and men) are viewed as more powerful, more fertile, stronger, better, sexier, and even nicer than their less attractive counterparts. (Psychological Reports, 1997.) Students who are seen as attractive by their teachers, will be perceived as smarter and get better grades. (Child Study Journal, 1975.) And it is beauty that is the inspiration of poets, composers, and artists, not kindness or intellect. Yet, beauty does nothing. It doesn't solve problems, challenge our intellect, heal the sick, cause change, or comfort the sad. Having said that, being pretty is, and has always been, a woman's best chance to marry well, and improve her social and economic position.

According to psychologist Judith Langlois, even infants come into the world equipped with the ability to discriminate and prefer the beautiful. Symmetrical faces cause them to coo, and asymmetrical faces make them cry. The four month-old baby grows up to become an adult who falls in love at first sight, and that sight is usually of an attractive person. And mothers of babies react to beauty by holding pretty babies longer, and answering their cries sooner.

So, why is beauty such an obsession? Where does its importance stem from? Why do we (women) care so much about how we look? Why do we spend billions of dollars on cosmetics, cosmetic surgery and dietary products? Why do we compare ourselves to other women, and envy those that we perceive to be more attractive? Why do we notice someone's hair color and features first, and why does the physical aspect remain in our mind's eye? Why do we undergo painful, and often dangerous, procedures to look younger, prettier, thinner?

The simple answer would be because we want to please men, or because we are victims of a massive conspiracy of the beauty industry to have us buy their products and procedures. But, it can't be that simple, because the pursuit of beauty transcends time, culture, civilization, and even age. So, knowing that our obsession with beauty has been around for as long as we have been man and woman, I agree with Nancy Etcoff, who states in her fascinating book, "Survival of the Prettiest", the desire to be beautiful is not learned, but an integral part of our nature and a universal part of human experience. She insists we are governed by circuits in the brain shaped by natural selection, and that attraction was devised to ensure the survival of the human race. Ultimately, even in the animal kingdom, beauty is rewarded by the preference of the opposite sex as a mating partner.

So, Ms. Etcoff says it shouldn't surprise us that "throughout human history people have scarred, painted, pierced, padded, stiffened, plucked, and buffed their bodies in the name of beauty ... During famines, Kalahari bushmen in Africa still use animal fats to moisture their skin ... and in 1715 riots broke out in France when the use of flour on the hair of aristocrats led to a food shortage." Today, In the United States, we spend more than twice as much money on personal care products and services as on reading material. In Brazil there are more Avon ladies than members of the army. (New York Times, July 7, 1995) Even Aristotle said beauty is a greater recommendation than any letter of introduction.

Every discipline, from the Kabbalah, Darwinian evolution, has tried to explain our obsession with beauty. The Kabbalah justifies a woman's need to be beautiful by describing her as the vessel that reflects light and harbors the soul. Kabbalist, Karen Berg, in "God Wears Lipstick," declares that it is "only natural that women need massages, manicured nails, hair-stylists and lovely clothes, for they are the vessels that house the soul," and just as we put beautiful flowers in an equally exquisite vase, our soul deserves to be housed in a lovely container. Again, in "Survival of the Prettiest", Etcoff explains Darwin's explanation of survival of the sexiest: "males focus more on pure physical appearance because appearance gives many clues about whether a woman is healthy and fertile."

But that was yesterday. Why do we continue to worship beauty and youth, (which are seen as one in the same), today? Looking maximally fertile, (by being a young woman and having the correct hip/waist ratio), is no longer a viable reason to be chosen as a love partner. Today, women can have children in their sixties through in vitro implantation, so, one would hope that men would begin to value qualities such as kindness and intellect, at least equally with beauty. And since neither our bodies nor our faces resemble the ones portrayed on the covers of magazines and billboards, it would also be nice if we could learn to accept our intrinsic qualities, and view our years of life as a source of pride.

One would think that with the advancement of psychology and technology, men and women alike would finally be able to see through the myths that surround beauty, and start to concentrate on the qualities that truly count. However, it takes instinct longer than technology to catch up with reality. And until that happens, most of us will be faced with what we consciously know to be true, and unconsciously have inherited through evolution.

> We have the choice to succumb to the universal and historical need to stay young and beautiful, or we can dig deep inside our psyches and our souls, and flaunt our other, inner qualities. For, after all, our response to beauty may be automatic, but our thoughts and behaviors are ultimately, and always, our choice.

For many, it won't be easy to fall in love with their inner beauty, nor will they want to do the work. One of the saddest statements I have ever heard about beauty came from Eleanor Roosevelt, one of my idols. When asked if she had any regrets, she answered, "Only to have been prettier." It is so sad to me, because she was able to make such a difference in the world, but beauty was something she couldn't do anything about. Doesn't seem fair, does it?

Beauty is pleasurable to behold in all of its forms, and I'm not advocating we stop appreciating it, only that we learn to acknowledge our enduring personality qualities as well.

Imagine the sight of a multicolored garden and the tones of autumn; the sound of the chords of your favorite instrument, or the laughter of children at play; the feel of cashmere on your skin, or your baby suckling at your breast; the smell of your lover's pillow, or of his signature cologne; the succulent taste of chocolate as you offer it to your lover; all are beautiful aspects of life that we would never want to give up!

It has taken me over sixty years, and the writing of this book, to understand why it has been so important, for me in particular, to be, and feel, beautiful. Once I was able to be completely honest with myself and put my fears into words, being beautiful took on a new meaning to me; maybe not less significant, but at least more comprehensible.

Today, I know that loving and being loved is beautiful;
that quiet self-esteem and security are beautiful; that
passion, and enthusiasm, and humility, and empathy
are beautiful. In contrast, arrogance is not beautiful,
nor is vanity, ego, selfishness, or insecurity.

At the same time, I share in the ambivalence of what my intellect
knows to be true, and the historical messages that are contained
in my genes. I hope to be able to reach a healthy balance as I get
older, so I can offer to my children and grandchildren a serene,
and happy face—not in spite of, but because of—the wrinkles I
have earned from laughter and tears.

Others Face their Mirrors

When it comes to looking beautiful, some people are more
obsessed than others. "Borrow, beg, but get a facelift," insists the
comedian, Joan Rivers. "Anything that can be lifted should be
lifted: anything that falls should be caught." She goes on to say it
is our duty to look great at every age, and is determined to fight old
age every way she can, with every illegal trick and every dishonest
blow. She plans to be buried with her plastic surgeon. (From Rivers'
conference tape: "Don't Count the Candles".)

Helen Gurley Brown, founding editor of Cosmopolitan, and author
of "Sex and the Single Girl", said she felt a combination of rage,
sorrow and disgust when she turned sixty-four and no longer felt
beautiful. (Today she is eighty and still does one hundred pushups
every day.) In her book, she said what she hated most was no
longer being perceived as adorable and cute, and being able to
afford the clothes that no longer looked good on her.

However, Paul Newman is frustrated by beauty's superficiality. "To work hard, as I've worked, to accomplish anything, and then have some yo-yo come up and say, 'Take off those dark glasses and let's have a look at those blue eyes' is really discouraging."

Even Plato had something to say about it: "The three wishes of every man: to be healthy, to be rich by honest means, and to be beautiful."

Oprah, who challenges the classical vision of beauty in her eponymous magazine, perceives fifty as her greatest hour. She has proven it by being more attractive, becoming thinner and richer than ever, and using her fabulous wealth and unlimited generosity to feed villages in Africa, and give away cars to everyone in her audience.

Letty Cottin Pogrebin, the brilliant feminist writer, now in her fifties, agrees. In, "Getting Over Getting Older", she writes that appearance no longer rules her life. "I concentrate on other people, and real problems, and how I might make a difference." She appreciates survival for its own sake and wants to look ahead to 2020, not with perfect vision, "but with gratitude for life, words, love, movement, memories, and all these hopes for the future."

What a thought! Those of us who have reached the third stage of life are the lucky ones, and we must never forget that. When we are frustrated because something in our body doesn't work or we can't zip up our tight jeans, let that be our mantra. We are the lucky ones! We get to be here!

Staying beautiful to the eye takes up a lot of time, costs large amounts of money, and is far from risk free. But, each of us has to decide how much time and money we want to devote to its pursuit. We need not spend more time than necessary debating what is more important, inner or outer beauty. I suggest we cultivate both, and put our own signature to our own individual creation.

As women, let's continue to become smarter, and kinder, and wiser. At the same time, let's not judge ourselves for caring about physical beauty nor hate other women who are younger or more beautiful than we. ("Lookism" is one of the most prevalent and least spoken about of prejudices.) By accepting ourselves and others, we will all truly be attractive to men, women, and children alike, and more importantly, to ourselves.

A Personal Story

There have been times when what I looked like was more important to me than to others. Just when I thought I had finally gotten to the point where I could proudly say, "I am more than my face. I am more than my body. I am proud of the wrinkles on my face because they reflect my life, my joys, my pains." I opened an e-mail from a person from my far-away past ... to be specific, from the high school football player who never paid attention to me. In a collective e-mail, he was inviting me to my thirty-year class reunion. It all came back! The popular boys, now men, weren't going to care if I was a wonderful mother, or if I had given speeches, or gone back to school. They were going to be looking me up and down, just like they did when I was a teenager, and they were going to find me lacking. I shouldn't care. I had outgrown such petty concerns, but the truth is, I did care.

It was about the same time that I was also diligently looking for a perfect dress to wear for my daughter Vannessa's wedding in Acapulco. In Spanish there is a dreaded word, el viejazo ... which means that one gets old all of a sudden. I was afraid the wedding guests might think I was a victim of el viejazo. My personal "all-of-sudden" was ten years, since most people had not seen me for over a decade. I know, I know. I was just the mother of the bride, not the bride. It wasn't important what I looked like. No one would care, except for me. I started to obsess.

I remember one day in particular. I went to my magnifying mirror and scrutinized my face up close. I saw new lines and creases I hadn't noticed the week before. I remember thinking, "Where did they come from?" Then reality hit, and I remembered that it was trash day. You may wonder why trash collection day would stay in my memory. Well, that moment represented an epiphany. I bent over my new, shiny, silver, tall trash can and saw a monster in the reflection and the monster was me! My skin appeared to be melting off my face and hanging down (only someone over fifty can identify). Then and there I knew it was urgent that I do something about my face before attending either of these events! Maybe I could get a facelift, or one of those new thread lifts. After all, I knew about all that stuff.

Before I could pick up the phone, (to make an appointment with the plastic surgeon who had just performed magic on my friend's face), it rang. It was my gynecologist. He said he was concerned about my pap smear; nothing to worry about, he insisted (sure!), but I should get in as soon as possible to take another one. All of a sudden those new jagged lines on my upper lip, and my sagging skin seemed very, very unimportant, as did the opinion of people I hadn't seen in decades, and probably wouldn't see again. All of a sudden I felt fear ... panic ... that my life was about to change radically, and that it was my turn to face the real fear of every woman's life. All of a sudden, all I wanted was for everything to be the same as it was when I discovered the monster on the trash can, before the phone rang. I would happily, willingly ... please, please ... gratefully accept my imperfections, just to be able to enjoy one more day on this glorious earth with my daughters.

Gracias a Dios; so it was. The laboratory had made a mistake. For a long, long time I paid more attention to all the little wonderful gifts of life (like breathing) and stopped paying attention to my mirror, and looking into the trash can. I did say for a while, didn't I?

Our Beauty Options

Today there are so many options, we can change anything we want. From lifting our faces and breasts to reshaping our feet, and even our vaginas; the pursuit of perfection is endless.

There is plastic surgery, wrinkle removal, weight loss surgery, umbilicoplasty, tummy tuck, thermage, skin resurfacing, sclerotherapy, scar revision, rhinoplasty, restylane, radiance, reconstructive surgery, cosmetic foot surgery, vaginal reconstruction, power assisted lipoplasty, otoplasty, nipple augmentation, micropigmentation, liposuction, lip augmentation, laser skin resurfacing, laser hair removal, hylaform, hand surgery, hair transplantation, forehead lift, fillers, fat injection, facelift, eyelid surgery, endermologie, deep microdermabrasion, collagen injection, chin augmentation, chemical peel, brow lift, breast reduction, breast lift, breast implants, breast enhancements, botox, sculptra, threadlifts, body lifts, body implants, blepharoplasty and autologous fat implants.

Without a doubt, if you don't like it, you can fix it! More than one million people had botox injections, and chemical peels last year; 461,000 had Restylane and Hylaform injections; 858,000 had microdermabrasion. Thanks to all these new fillers, we live in a brave new world, where we might never have wrinkles, sagging jowls, or crows feet ... ever.

According to a recent edition of Vogue magazine "With the stigma gone, and replaced with excitement about these new in and out procedures to look younger, men and women are showing up everywhere, proud of their black and blue telltale signs." In fact, the author goes on to say, "instead of being ashamed, people don't mind looking scary, and happily parade around town with bruising or swelling."

The Vogue article on the new attitude towards reversing aging continues, "In the rush to look better, men and women don't mind going out looking like hell ... there are bruised, swollen, and laser-burned faces turning up at dinner parties, at the chicest restaurants and in corporate boardrooms ... a few pinpricks are as normal on the Upper East Side as a Maltese ... as they are in Beverly Hills. Going to a convention or a party bleeding from botox injections is a small price to pay for the fountain of youth, and no more shocking than dark roots used to be!"

Please Note: Being beautiful and being rewarded for it is not a social evil. In fact, without beauty, and all its forms, ours would be a very drab world.

The Thing Is ...

The thing is, you are beautiful. Whoever you are, no matter what you look like, your beauty lies within, in your spirit and your smile.

You may not have any wrinkles, and you may have a china doll face with lips that curve in just such a way, but if your heart is dull and your mind anxious or angry, then your beauty will attract only emptiness. As Letty Cottin Pogrebin says in Getting Over Getting Older, "What good is it to turn fifty with an unwrinkled face if there's no light behind the eyes, no passion in the voice, no ideas happening inside the head? ... When we die, do we want people to exclaim, 'She looked ten years younger' or do we want them to say, 'She lived a great life?'"

Yes, it's your choice. There are options that range from the natural to the artificial; from ingredients you can grow in your garden to exotic and new technological miracles; from cremes that take minutes to apply to surgeries that take months to heal; from changes that are only subtly noticeable to those that turn you into someone you barely recognize in the mirror.

> The message I send to you, to myself, to my daughters, is the following: if we are conscious of what we put into our minds, spirits and bodies; if we are enthusiastic, passionate and positive; if we focus more on others than ourselves, the beauty will certainly shine through our souls.

At the same time, I understand the evolutionary need for us to remain youthful and beautiful and the pressure imposed upon us by the messages of the media. I am not immune to such pressures and have to deal with my own fears and ambivalence which as you know originated when I was a child. I have studied the more invasive procedures as viable options, and I invite you to go to my web site, lindanacif.com where I outline the latest in lunchtime procedures and cosmetic surgeries.

Natural Beauty Secrets

Witch hazel tightens your skin and shrinks pores: apply to clean, dry skin with a cotton ball.

Use drug store eye shadows to camouflage dark circles: add yellow eye shadow to your foundation and pat around eyes.

A small amount of beige eye shadow on the center of your eyelids makes your eyes look bigger. Put on top of your regular eye shadow and then blend in.

Take a cough drop containing menthol or eucalyptus because it will end your food cravings...and give you good breath.

Drink at least a gallon of water a day. This helps to flush wastes from the blood, reduce constipation, and prevent toxins from building up in fat cells.

Use beeswax and honey to soothe and protect your skin. Honey sooths skin and firms tissue by plumping cells up with water. Beeswax helps protect the skin naturally against bacteria because it contains antibacterial propolis.

Try hazelnut oil for softer skin. Its oil deeply penetrates and softens the skin.

Juniper and rosemary oils increase circulation, decongest sluggish and under-active tissues, and stimulate the body's metabolism.

Although Jojoba oil is expensive, it is worth it. Add it to all of your natural crèmes because it will protect them from going rancid.

A facial pack once a week keeps pimples and blackheads away. Not to be confused with a facial mask, it is an intensive healing treatment that makes use of moist heat to remove deep-seated impurities.

Here is a great facial pack for oily skin: 2bsp. Ground oatmeal, 1/2 tsp. wheat-germ oil, 2-4 tbsp. hot sage tea, 1 tbsp. ground flaxseed. Apply the mixture when still warm and relax!

The sun wrinkles us prematurely. Remember, there is no safe tan. You'll need to go to the drugstore and buy a sunscreen with an SPF of at least 15 for maximum sun protection.

If you do get burned in the sun, apply a thin coat of yogurt or aloe-vera gel to sun burned areas.

Spray pure lavender water on sun-damaged skin to keep skin hydrated, help prevent peeling, and promote the regeneration of cells.

Diluted St. John's wort oil is wonderful and soothing if you have been too long in the sun.

Strawberries make a great skin mask because they are rich in vitamin C. They also contain sulfur, which has cleansing and anti-inflammatory properties. Their natural fruit acids and enzymes exfoliate, and produce a radiant result. Wash 4-5 medium-sized strawberries in lukewarm water and dry with a cloth. Mash the fruit with a fork, and add 2 tbsp. heavy cream and 1 tsp. honey. When applying any mask always leave space around the mouth, eyes and eyebrows. Leave most masks on for 20-30 minutes.

Prepare natural masks before you need them and refrigerate. By doing that, you will always be prepared when you get that unexpected invitation from someone wonderful.

To help prevent split ends, rub olive oil into the ends of your hair 2-3 times per week. For best results, leave the oil on overnight and wash it out in the morning.

Prepare an herbal hair rinse the same way you make an herbal tea. Pour a cup of boiling water over a teaspoon of herbs. Steep for 10 minutes, then strain. Massage the rinse into the scalp and leave on the hair without rinsing. Dry naturally. Sage, chamomile, and birch-leaf (only for dark hair) will repair damaged hair and nourish the hair follicle and promote healthy growth.

For rough hands, add vitamins E and A, (with German-chamomile or calendula), to a water-based cream.

Protect your skin from winter weather. Apply a thick coat of a pure oil-based cream to your skin, and then add sweet-almond oil, Jojoba oil, beeswax, and rose water.

For dry skin, add 10 drops of calendula essential oil, 15 drops Aloe Vera concentrate, and 2 drops coriander-seed essential oil to 2 oz. of cream.

For broken capillaries, add 10 drops German-chamomile oil, or 10 drops vitamin-E oil, or 10 drops blue-cypress essential oil

You can make all homemade, natural cosmetics last longer by adding Jojoba oil, which is a liquid wax, and therefore does not go rancid.

When gardening, don't forget to apply a thick, oil-based cream to your hands and fingernails, so that you can remove the dirt easily.

For wrinkles on the neck, use a wrap with 2 tsp. of warm, unrefined peanut oil, and 4-6 drops of rose-hip-seed oil, letting it work overnight.

You can eat or use avocados topically for moisturizing, preventing the formation of liver spots, and protecting the skin from sun damage.

Eat lots of fruit and foods rich in vitamins A, B, D and E, and lecithin, to maintain silky, beautiful skin.

Cellulite is the accumulation of fat, water, and waste that gets trapped beneath the skin. So, avoid caffeine, and reduce your intake of salt.

Massage yourself! Self-massage done routinely can alleviate aches and pains, prevent disease, and enhance the effect of other healing methods. It is also proven to be a remedy for fatigue, insomnia, muscle tension, muscle weakness, joint pain, and skin problems.

Depending on your need, while administering self massage, you can rub in a circular motion, (to stimulate circulation and release muscle tension), or you can knead (use a little warm natural vegetable oil as a lubricant as if you were working with bread dough) or vibrate (use rhythmic knocking or light slapping with flat hands), to improve blood circulation and relax muscles.

Your Natural Beauty Shopping List:

For massage:
Sweet-almond oil (appropriate for every skin type)
Grape seed oil (for acne and greasy skin)

Jojoba oil (for sensitive skin, blend with other oils, since it prevents them from going rancid.)
Sesame oil (good for all skin types, and especially for psoriasis, eczema, and arthritis)

For weather-protection:
Beeswax
German-Chamomille
Calendula
Carrot-seed oil
Rose water
Borax
Aloe Vera concentrate
Vitamin E oil
Juniper oil
Rosemary oil

Anti-wrinkle Crème:
Apricot-kernal oil
Avocado oil
Lanolin
Pure honey

Anti-cellullite Oils:
Hazelnut oil
Cinnamon-leaf essential oil
Juniper essential oil
Rosemary essential oil
Cypress essential oil
Orange essential oil
Lemon essential oil
Lime essential oil

Facial Pack:
French green clay
Thyme essential oil
Hot sage tea

Linda's Subtle Beauty Secrets

Nothing, absolutely nothing, keeps your looks and enhances your beauty more than simple, regular exercise! Walk, bike, swim, dance ... do anything you enjoy.

A beautiful, responsive smile and a positive attitude are what will attract people to you in the long haul.

Knowledge of what is going on in the world creates an intriguing and compelling you.

Being more interested than interesting makes YOU irresistible.

Being confident, in contrast to being needy, is what men find attractive.

Always walk with your shoulders back and head high. You will look young, and people will be intrigued by why you are so confident.

Remember the law of scarcity: we all want we can't have, so be illusive and not always available, and you will appear more desirable.

Be kind to everyone. Trust me, men want to be around women who treat others well.

Forget about yourself and focus on others. Most people don't notice if you have had a bad hair day, because they are worrying about their own hair.

Meditate. You will be surprised how beautiful you look after you do. You will have a special aura that others will gravitate towards.

Be passionate, enthusiastic, and excited about life. Just as you like to be around people that have these traits, so does everyone else.

Be curious. Ask lots of questions. And look into his eyes when you do.

Watch beautiful women. Notice how they move, how they talk, how they hold their bodies. Then, imitate them. Act as if you felt beautiful and others will see you as beautiful. Guaranteed.

In Conclusion

Yes, the search for beauty and the pleasure derived upon admiring it are not going to go away, nor should we want them to. Imagine a world where we don't enjoy looking at the peacock or where we punish the spectacular bird for having and exhibiting its colorful and gorgeous plumage! Imagine a world without ornaments to adorn ourselves, or without fashion options to portray our unique style. In other words, imagine a world without beauty. It would be a very bland and boring place indeed.

> However we can decide to look beyond the outside image and learn to value the qualities that make a true difference in our world. We can broaden our definition of what is beautiful to encompass all shapes, ages, and cultures.

Beautiful women come into being every day, and it's not in the surgeon's office, but in circles of friends, and laughter and in silences of self-knowing. So shine your teeth and buff up your butt. Get rid of that extra chin if you like, and put a little color in your hair. You've got a style all your own; have fun with it. Just remember, fun starts with a smile, and so does beauty. You can't buy that in a bottle.

"To know how to grow old
is the master work of wisdom."

~ Henri Aniel

Chapter Two

Age

(2002)

Dear Vannessa,

So, how lucky can I be? In one unforgettable day, I was a witness to two occasions that would mold and change your life, and at the same time, stay embedded in my heart forever. It is hard for you to understand how difficult it is to be apart from you, and only be able to participate in your life with my imagination. But today, I was there! I was there in the morning when you greeted your eager, tiny students for the first time, and at the stroke of midnight, when you were carried away in a chariot by prince charming. I was there to admire how well you executed every detail, and at the same time how you forgot detail, and gave yourself to the moment. I was there to hear parents acclaim your unique teaching talent, and the courier announce the invitation to a princess. I was there ... as I wish I always could be.

You created "Choice Time" so that children could choose from a myriad of art forms to express not only their talent, but their emotions before they were able to articulate the words. What an immense gift to offer a child! By offering them "choice" you are tacitly telling them they don't have to look outside for answers or approval, for the truth can only come from inside. I believe when they grow up, they will take this valuable lesson, albeit unconscious, with them. These empowered children will understand that only they have the right to choose the strokes and colors with which they want to paint their lives, and the music that makes their hearts sing.

It was in this very room, in the house that I shared with your father and sisters, that I too taught women about their choices. Maybe if we had a teacher like Miss Vanne when we were younger, we would already have known that choice is a God-given legacy to be experienced by everyone. When I saw what was once my sterile conference room, I couldn't believe my eyes. You had converted this space into a wondrous haven for pre-school children. Multi colored, plastic covered little tables with four equally tiny chairs, perfectly organized, reachable cubicles filled with more art crafts than I knew existed, colorful signs everywhere with the words, "love, compassion, honesty, understanding, forgiveness," words that symbolized your beliefs, and that would prepare your young students to live in a kinder, more forgiving world.

And you already had a waiting list, because as I learned later, "Vanne" is one of the favorite "Misses" at the prestigious Litton school. Watching you greet the parents and hug your first-time students as you handed them their color-coordinated plastic aprons that were held on the rainbow-colored hooks, made me marvel at your creativity and loving demeanor.

I thought I was watching so closely, yet even I, your mother, didn't realize that you had transformed into such a capable woman. With each year, you have become more multi-faceted. Few people at such a young age possess the wisdom to know where their bliss lies, much less the courage to follow it. It takes most of us a lifetime to know what we want, and when we discover our true calling later in life, we wrongly believe it is too late, or we are too old to realize our dreams.

And tonight you lived the moment that dreams and fairy tales are made of. I wasn't aware Aureo was going to ask you for your hand in marriage, but Vivianne took me to the side, and secretly shared with me the romantic plan. We would all be at your Dad's house, sharing our impressions of the Choice Time inauguration. Aureo was going to send a friend of his, dressed as a courier, who would blow a horn, unravel a long piece of parchment and read a dictate from "Prince Aureo" for "Princess Vannessa."

And so it was. We were all sitting in the living room, when the courier arrived. You should have seen your face when the unexpected messenger, dressed in velvet and lace, invited you to a royal encounter with the prince of your heart, and instructed you to be properly attired and ready in half an hour.

When the courier left, and after jumping up and down and hugging each other, we all ran down to your dressing room to get the princess costume you had worn for a costume party. We knew it would be the perfect dress, but you had loaned it to a friend and she broke the zipper. Now, what to do? What to do? I remembered the gown that I wore to Jenny's wedding had been cleaned and was still hanging in the closet. We quickly stripped the plastic off of it, and you put it on, and oh my gosh ... it fit you perfectly. Wow! The princess would wear my dress to the ball.

Soon Aureo arrived on your street, in a shiny, pumpkin shaped Cinderella carriage, pulled by a car. He was dressed in a velvet, blue, prince's costume, trimmed in white lace and gold embroidery. Your real "Principe Azul" beckoned you to join him in his carriage, where he was to take you to a romantic hideaway and give you the ring you proudly showed us when you returned. Yes, I was there, to wave you on, and to applaud your choices.

Miss Vanne, I admire you so. I can only imagine how you will prosper in the future if you keep listening to your heart, and most importantly, act on your intuition.

As I get older, and perhaps because we are separated by thousands of miles, I feel a growing need to share with you, (and your sisters), thoughts and conclusions that can only be derived after having lived many decades. It is my ardent hope that on one of "those" days, (you know, the ones when we feel confused, or sad, or scared), my written words will give you hope, or perspective, or at least, food for thought. When we are young, we are often busy and take so many things for granted ... less aware, less conscious, even less grateful. That is just the nature of youth! So, indulge your mami, as she feels a little more sentimental than usual, and uses love as her lifeline to express her thoughts.

Vanne, I see life as a play. You have stepped forward fully into the first act of your life, just as I am stepping into the third act of mine. And, just like in a play, in order for a performance to be memorable, every act must be significant and meaningful ... complete unto itself. And so it is with our lives.

How sad that so many older men and women forsake the third act of their lives, and use it as a resting place to accumulate resentment or to wait for the curtain to go down. However, the truth remains, once again, as in a play, the act that permits us to tie everything together, the act that allows us to learn from our mistakes and transcend, is the third and last one. As the protagonists of our lives, we owe it to ourselves and to future generations, to incorporate what we have learned, and share it with them. We must create a masterpiece of this act, for it is the one that will be remembered.

Marriage and children were my raison d'être in the first four decades of my life; staying emotionally, physically, and spiritually healthy are my driving forces now. As you watch me, please realize that someday you will draw upon this early story that you are living to create your later and most pivotal performance.

Every time I watch unwavering athletes compete in the Senior Olympics; every time I enjoy the presence of a witty and enthusiastic older sister; every time I work out with, and admire, the sculptured body of a woman in her sixties or seventies; every time I spy an elderly couple giving each other a big, slobbery kiss on the lips; in other words, every time I observe someone in their advanced years doing what they did in the beginning of their lives ... and yes, every time I feel sexual passion arise in my body ... I know the perceived limits of aging are lies. Our bodies and our hearts continue to yearn for movement, for touch, for connection, for passion, and for love, until the day we die.

While you, in your first act, are very caught up in the romance of life, I, too, am at a crossroads and a kind of romance as well. As you begin, my daughter, I also savor the opportunity to choose to begin again. Who knows? Maybe in yet another country with a self-realized partner, or becoming an expert on sex after sixty, or doing something impractical like learning to belly dance, or humanitarian like going to Brazil to work with Habitat for Humanity, or just having fun ... like riding my bike through the unpaved streets of the Yucatan peninsula. Nothing will be a wrong choice, for whatever I decide, I know I will return with more lessons and more wisdom to "remember, remember, remember," and share with you.

What a different sort of life you and I have before us. We could both live to be ninety, or even a hundred. Imagine, Vannessa, someday, you will once again wear my dress, but it will be the dress of age. And you will wear it as beautifully as you wear the dress of youth; with your distinct style.

Yes, my darling, you were a beautiful thing to behold when you were carried away by your Prince Charming, but you were even more beautiful when you returned, with the knowledge that you had to prepare for the following day when your ideas, your lessons, your passion, your inner beauty would be shared with your students. Cultivate that seed of beauty that is within and radiates your inner beauty, so that it blooms even more gloriously when you are over fifty, sixty and seventy.

Once again I return to the United States and take with me all that you have become. I hope to be worthy of the love and confidence that you bestow on me every trip. I know that Aureo will perceive your true beauty, as your students do, as I do, and you will both live in the kingdom of mutual strength and empowerment. I will miss you, but soon it will be time to exercise another choice; that of choosing your wedding dress, and once again I will be there! I can't wait!!

Awaiting and knowing that you will continue to give me many more magical moments,

tu mami

The What and How of Age

Because of the emphasis and importance our society has bestowed on youth, getting older was always something I feared. The women I observed when I was growing up, who were probably younger than I am today, seemed to be resigned to looking back on their youth as their best years, and have given up on their futures. They appeared to me to be asexual, tired; reconciled to their plight. Comparing life to a play, these passionless women are merely living off stage, waiting for the curtain to come down.

But, today, everything has changed! Women of a "certain age" are more secure, more confident, more willing to risk, and more sexual than in any previous generation. I needlessly wasted years worrying about a deterioration that never happened, for today, well into my sixth decade, I have never been happier, or more in love with life. It's not that I am wise, or know everything. It is because I now know I have so much to learn, and have the time to discover and savor the sacred process of life.

We, who are fortunate enough to have lived 60+ years, have the opportunity to dispel the myth of aging. Contrary to what I lived and feared, the truth is, emotionally, we can revel in who we have become, and no longer have to look for approval, or pretend to be who we aren't. Hormonally, we are finally at peace; no longer having to worry about fluctuating moods, pregnancy, PMS, or menopause. Sexually, experience has taught us about our bodies, and maturity permits us to ask for what we need and want. Spiritually, we can embrace the unknown, open to new ideas, and internal growth. Physically, we can carry our weight in the world, stronger, and with more pride than ever.

In fact, one of the reasons for this book is to put into black and white, the truth of what it is really like to be an older woman! Of course, that is if we do the work!!!

Daring to Ask The Questions

Why do we age?

Do we have to accept the so-called symptoms of aging; loss of muscle and bone mass, increase in body fat, insulin resistance, decline in strength, energy, and our immune system?

Must we be punished for having lived long lives?

Do we have a choice on how we look, feel, and live the last years of our lives?

Although we have to get older, do we have to get old?

Can we reverse the aging process?

More importantly, is there anything we can do today, (regardless of how young or old we are), to assure continued health, strength, stamina, and enthusiasm?

These were questions I needed to answer for myself. I witnessed the slow decline of my parent's health, and did not want to end my days in pain and agony as they did. But, if I had to accept the inevitable destruction of my mind and body, so be it. However, if there was something, anything I could do to enjoy my life until I took my last breath, I was going to find out about it ... and do it!

The answers to these questions permit me to be excited and optimistic about my next thirty years. The advice I consciously follow and live, every waking hour of my life, confirms the veracity of this research. I invite you to join me, and thousands of women as we convert every stage of our lives into a masterpiece.

Yes, it's never too early or too late to live in conscious
joy and health, yet staying "young" takes commitment,
dedication, and discipline.   But, just think of the
alternative, if we don't do the work!

Why Do We Age?

Scientists and researchers are working hard to find out why we age
and die. And whether we opt to believe it is because of telomeres,
(those little caps on our DNA that keep getting shorter as we age),
or free radicals, (molecules that roam our bodies stealing electrons
and damaging our tissues), or chronic inflammation, (cells that
enter the arteries and activate fat cells to cause insulin resistance),
or a combination of all of the above, all scientists agree there are
things we can do to slow down the deterioration process.

Our bodies are in a constant mode of repair, but this rate slows
as we age, and inner and outer beauty begin to show the signs.
This process of cell renewal is controlled by our anabolic rate ...
the rate and efficiency at which our 100 trillion cells renew and
repair themselves. Think of our anabolic rate as building up, or
as our repair budget. When we are young and healthy, our repair
budget is extremely high, which is why we are able to look, feel,
and perform at peak efficiency. It's almost like we wake up a new
person every day. However, as we age, this rate begins to decline.
We begin to look and feel older. The catabolic rate, (the rate at
which we break down), exceeds the anabolic rate. So, if we keep
our anabolic rate up, and our catabolic rate down, doesn't it make
sense that we could continue to live vibrant lives?

> The question is, how do we enhance our anabolic rate? The answer is, by avoiding cell damage, and supporting cell growth and repair, and we can achieve this through diet and life style.

By feeding our cells healthy, organic, food that is alive; by lowering our levels of the "death hormone" cortisol, by moving and stretching our bodies, and surrounding ourselves with love, we CAN live the 120 years that most of us are genetically designed to live. Our bodies are engineered to take us all the way to the end, and we don't have to let them break down along the way.

Yes, my daughters and sisters, the truth will set us free; free from the dread of aging, free to grow and stretch and expand, and, of course, to jump, knowing the joy will follow. The following are ten facts ... not theories ... I discovered. Anyone of them, if put into practice, can change your life!!!

The Ten Truths

1. We Do Not Have To Degenerate!
What we previously took to be the inevitable ravages of aging are actually poor lifestyle choices and habits.

2. It's All About Balance.
We can finish a marathon, remember where we put our keys, have a toned body, learn a foreign language, take a bike tour through Europe, and have multiple orgasms at any age, if we learn to balance our time, our commitments, our emotions, our food intake, and our hormones.

3. We Have Choices!

The choices we opt for today will make the difference tomorrow between mere survival, (perhaps in a nursing home), or enjoying a full, healthy, and eventful life.

4. Certain Physical And Psychological Symptoms Are Age Related, But They Are Not Age Inevitable.

Do not accept your complaints as inevitable. Symptoms are messages from our bodies for us to change something. If we continue to deny or avoid the warnings, the symptoms will eventually overwhelm us, and take over our lives.

5. How We Age Is About Every Day, Consistent, Small Decisions.

It's all about converting good, conscious decisions into unconscious, daily habits. Bad habits, not genetic defects, catch up with us over time.

6. It Is Never Too Late To Reverse Our Biological Age.

We can remake ourselves and recharge our lives at any age, but the earlier we begin, the healthier and longer our life span will be.

7. We Cannot Live Longer Than We Are Genetically Programmed To Live.

But we can die earlier due to bad life style habits. The difference between genetic aging and biological aging is that we have no control over the former, and complete control over the latter. In other words, genetics dictate how long we will live, but it is our lifestyle habits that will permit us to reach that age, or die sooner.

8. Menopause Marks The End Of Our Child Bearing Years, Not The Death Of Intimacy Or Sexual Pleasure.

Our ability to enjoy our sexual selves in later life is governed by our desire to continue to experiment and an understanding of how our bodies are changing. If we learn how to keep our vaginas moist, and our libidos activated through use, BHRT, (Bio-Identical Hormone Replacement Therapy), and tightening of our PC muscle by doing Kegels, we will be physically able to have orgasms until our 90's!

9. Every Single Thought And Nutrient We Put Into Our Bodies Will Show Up Later In Life, Either As Statements Of Health Or Disease, Joy Or Depression, Beauty Or Plainness, Enthusiasm Or Bitterness, Passion Or Frigidity.
By living consciously, in contrast to mechanically, we will learn to honor our bodies as the only vehicles we have to go through life. Being aware it is our choices, more than our genes, that will permit us to live lives of health, vigor, and joy.

10. The Meanings We Give To Aging Will Affect Every Decision We Make, And Every Aspect Of Our Lives.
Depending on a myriad of factors, such as health, emotional wounds, the presence or absence of a support group, how active or inactive we are, and our spiritual connection, we will either embrace this stage as a wondrous opportunity, or reject it with resignation.

Linda's Natural Aging Prevention Secrets

Many of my "secrets" will be explained in more detail throughout the book, but here is a summary of what you will find in each chapter.

Exercise: If there is an anti-aging pill, it has to be exercise. Exercise helps maintain vital hormones, increases self esteem and oxygen utilization, allows muscles and tendons to be flexible, prolongs life, and improves mental function by inducing the growth of capillaries in the brain.

Meditate: Meditators shift their brain activity to different areas of the cortex; brain waves in the stress-prone right, frontal cortex move to the calmer left, frontal cortex. This mental shift decreases the negative effects of stress, mild depression, and anxiety.

Eat fresh, organic, food: Unprocessed fruits and vegetables are loaded with nutrients and phytochemicals for cleansing and rejuvenating cells. Bitter greens will tone and detoxify the liver. Grains, such as brown rice, oats, barley, rye, and corn, are high in B-complex vitamins, vitamin E, and zinc, which are potent anti-cancer agents.

Eat sea vegetables: Arame, dulse, kelp, hijiki, nori and wakame can be used in dozens of ways, and only a little is needed. They are powerhouses of minerals such as iron, iodine, and calcium, and the best source of important trace minerals.

Eat grapes: They contain three compounds that may help reduce the risk of hardening of the arteries, and are natural antioxidants. (Eat the seeds and save the money on expensive grape seed extract.)

Eat Berries: They strengthen the blood vessels, as well as normalize blood pressure.

Drink red grape juice and plenty of water: The first contains flavonoids, which protect against heart attacks, and the latter flushes out toxins.

Get 7-8 hours of continuous sleep: Rebuild what you depleted in the day, give the brain a chance to consolidate memory, and rebalance hormones and brain chemicals. Nothing is more effective than a good night's sleep to restore body and soul.

Be grateful and count your blessings: People with a bright outlook may live longer than those who take a dimmer view. These are the best defenses against cortisol, the stress hormone.

Keep Cool: Cooking at high temperatures creates changes in molecules that may not be properly used by the body, and can create toxic substances within foods. When possible, eat well-washed, raw, organic fruit and vegetables.

Watch your weight: Cutting calories may do more than help you shed excess weight. Already proven in mice, and actively being studied in humans, it appears that calorie restriction may also slow down the aging process.

Love: Those who age successfully and resist illness, are those who have close relationships; be it family, friends, church affiliation, or a pet.

Play mind games: Keeping your mind young can slow the onset of dementia or Alzheimer's. Just like muscles, brain cells are dynamic structures.

Enjoy sex as often as possible: Sex reduces risk of heart disease and depression, relieves pain, improves posture, reduces stress, and is great exercise since it works the pelvis, thighs, buttocks, and arms.

Avoid:

    Smoking
    Animal protein
    Refined white flour
    Sugar
    Coffee
    Soft Drinks
    Alcohol

Anti-Aging Herbs:

    Burdock: eliminates toxins in the body.

Devil's claw: relieves aches and pains by dispelling uric acid.

Horsetail: replaces silica in the joints, and repairs cartilage.

Meadowsweet: It's what aspirin is made out of, and helps to control pain and reduce inflammation.

Garlic: balances blood pressure if taken as part of a preventative health strategy against high blood pressure.

Bearberry: nourishes the walls of the blood vessels in order to keep their elasticity. It's also used to replace lost silica in the joints, thereby promoting the re-growth and repair of cartilage.

Green tea: reduces risk of stroke and helps protect against rectal and pancreatic cancer because it contains polyphenols, chemicals that act as powerful antioxidants.

Anti-Aging Supplements of the future: (I take today)

Alpha Lipoic Acid (ALA): It's a natural and powerful antioxidant that helps the body use glucose. Food contains only a tiny amount of ALA, so supplements are recommended. A dose of 10 mg to 50 mg a few times a week is beneficial.

Carnosine: This is not only a powerful antioxidant, it appears to be able to extend the lifespan of cells, rejuvenate aging cells, and inhibit the toxic effects of DNA damage, therefore having the potential to prolong our lives. A daily dosage of 50 mg to 100 mg daily seems appropriate.

Resveratrol: The compound that makes red wine a healthy

drink; it may also hold one of the secrets to longevity by restricting our appetite.

Neuro Replete: A potent combination of neurotransmitters and amino acid therapy that relieves depression and anxiety, and helps prevent memory loss.

Tailor supplements to your current needs: For example, saw palmetto and pumpkin seed oil for prostate trouble; kelp, black cohosh and evening primrose oil for menopause. The three G's, (ginko biloba, ginseng, and garlic), for mental clarity, vigor, and tissue health. For the heart, use hawthorn and coenzyme Q10 as well as vitamins C and E, flax seed oil, and fish oils. Burdock, and dandelion root cleanse the blood. To rejuvenate the colon, look for acidophilus, laterosporus, and ground flax seeds.

Making Our Own Decisions

Each of us will have to make our own decisions about how we age, and how much time we want to dedicate attempting to put time back. Below are some exercises that will help you to clarify how you feel about yourself and what is most important to you. As always, no judgments; just sincere attempts at self-awareness to guide us through this unknown passage called aging.

The first step is to visualize yourself exactly as you want to be in ten years, then twenty, then thirty years. The purpose of visualizing is to clear out any negative thoughts or fears, and permit us to be our best selves. Anatomists have proven that images affect every cell in the body. So, close your eyes and visualize the person that you want to be, and already are. See, feel, taste, enjoy being the person you want to be, and believe you are already she.

Don't be ashamed to imagine the most brilliant, luscious, fit woman you can conjure up. Know that it is you, and it's only a matter of time and space to achieve your vision.

Questions:

> What does she look like?
> What is she wearing?
> Where is she?
> What is she doing?
> Whom is she with?

These visualizations are about what you see.

Now, combine what you see with affirmations, which are about what you say. When you do this, you will be preparing your own, very special path, and becoming strong from within. Together with visualization, affirmations are the language of possibility and change. They literally stimulate our nervous system to go beyond our limitations.

The ancient book of wisdom, the Tao Te Ching, says, "The words we choose are the seeds of our future realities. Those who identify with success will meet with success; those who identify with failure are welcomed with failure" (Working Out Working Within, The Tao on Inner Fitness Through Sports, by Jerry Lynch, Chungliang Al Huang, and Al Chung-Liang Huang.)

Upon preparing your affirmation, remember it is a strong, positive statement that is always phrased in the present, and states what you want, never what you don't want. By saying, "I am not fat, and not eating sugar anymore," your brain only registers, "I am fat and eating sugar." Instead say, " I am healthy and eating food that nourish me."

Here are some examples of affirmations you can use:

> "I am proud of my achievements, and reflect this by my stance and tone of voice."

> "My wrinkles reflect exquisite moments of sexual pleasure, and I display them with pride."

> "I am completely in control of my life and loving it!"

> "I can think clearly and solve my own problems."

> "I have more than enough time and live in the now."

> "I am attracting a loving, secure man who appreciates my experience and wisdom."

> "I am in the ocean laughing and effortlessly jumping the waves with my grandchildren."

> "I am finishing a half marathon surrounded by the applause of my daughters."

When we combine the visualization with the affirmations in my conferences, when the participants open their tear-filled eyes, they already look different.

It is only when you literally see, feel, and hear yourself the way you want to be, that you will recognize yourself as you truly are, and take the action necessary to meet your image. You will experience the physical strength, emotional zest, and mental power that will bring you back to your authentic self.

Maybe that's the answer to the mystery of why we have become a nation of obese, stressed, and tired people, working at jobs we hate, and yearning for the weekend.

We do a lot of things. We have more than we need. Yet, we haven't taken the time to be.

Now that you are strong, energetic, happy, and excited about this stage, and every stage of your life, here are the four elements to create who you already are. Begin today, because movement creates momentum.

Linda's Visualization

Ten years from now: I'm seventy-two. I am so very grateful for my blessings, and I give thanks to be alive. I'm still strong and healthy, and I stand tall, proud of myself, my accomplishments, my children and grandchildren, and even of my wrinkles. I am giving courses and changing the way women my age and younger feel about getting older. In Acapulco where it began, we are forming a community of sexy, vital, and happy women who are following their dreams, are mentors to their children, and recognize that all children are their children. We are sharing our hearts and thoughts, power walking and exercising on the beach, creating ceremonies of rites of passage, eating healthy, delicious food, and loving our lives. I am making sufficient money to sustain myself, and to be generous with my daughters, and the charities I hold dear.

In that visualization, sometimes I am traveling around the world with a like-minded man who understands my need to be free. We are working together to make this a more just and humane world. Together we are empowering both men and women to take control of the quality of their lives. A like-minded man, not just concerned about his physical looks, but with his spirit and his heart. Together we write books, give speeches, and share tantric sex. I can see my three daughters looking at each other with a big smile because they know Mami is completely happy at last.

Ask Yourself This:

What were you told when you were growing up about aging and growing older?

What do you feel and do when you see someone over eighty?

Are you curious about where they've been and who they are, or do you pretend to not see them?

What do you look forward to with the passage of time?

What do you fear, if anything, as you age?

Do you believe you can control the quality and quantity of your life?

What are you doing today so you will be healthy and strong when you're over sixty?

How much do you know about exercise and nutrition?

What excuses do you give so you won't have to change your negative habits?

Whom do you admire? Who is a mentor for you who is sixty-plus years old?

If you knew that if you changed your nutritional and lifestyle habits you would live twenty years longer, would you?

How do you want to be remembered?

Age is as age does. We grow older, and if we choose, we also can grow wiser, more beautiful, and happier with each passing day. What I am about to share with you has brought me back to myself; a new and wiser self, who is more confident, compassionate, assertive, and happier than I ever imagined. I have learned many lessons, and am open and excited to discover the ones I have yet to learn.

> The myth of age is one of human impotency, yet nothing could be further from the truth. The truth lies nestled in our will. It is our will to push back, to take up the tools of a healthy lifestyle and grateful consciousness to cultivate the garden of the rest of our lives.

I mean for us to marshal to our defense a robust sense of self that says, "I will decide my worth and my true youth." In doing so, we change ourselves, and we change our society. We become leaders to those younger than us and to our peers.

At the same time, we never forget that we are finite, and appreciate the beauty of every sunrise and sunset, the laughter of our grandchildren, the heartfelt conversations with our friends, and all the small, wonderful stuff of life. If we are ever tempted to forget and focus more on our wrinkles than our blessings, we are reminded that death is always around the corner, and we don't have the luxury to waste our time on the little stuff. So, let's focus on what we have, not on what we are lacking, and treasure being alive and be oh, so very grateful for the opportunity to become better every day.

As we age, we become warriors for the land of energy, joy, and serenity. We battle anxiety. We battle messages from the media and unthinking individuals. We gather within ourselves the spirit of life, and we look into our own eyes with the enthusiasm of winners. Our faces bear, more than anything, the creases of our smiles as we greet a new day.

"Nothing is static,
each a new beginning."

~ Tao Te Ching

$\mathcal{S}tress$

(1990 and 1991)

My decision to leave Mexico and the challenges to adapting
to being North American again.

My Three Daughters,

It is so vital to me that you understand why I have to
leave. Actually, maybe it is just as important for me that
you know why I married and stayed, since you have all
said you don't understand why two people with such
different backgrounds ever married at all.

It saddens me that although your father and I shared so many happy moments, the memories that will remain in your hearts will be of our recent tears and anger. You don't remember how much your father and I loved each other, or how much I wanted, and believed, that I could turn myself inside out to become an "abnegada", (self-denying), Lebanese wife.

In this longer than usual letter, I will do my best to explain to you why I chose your father, why I accepted the life that I did, why I ultimately have to leave, and even stranger, why I would do it all over again. As always, I will try to be as honest and fair as I can, with the hope that you will not only understand me, but perhaps, your father, as well.

I was eighteen when I embarked on my adventure to Mexico City. All alone, with only a list of addresses that my father had given me, I visited the first person on the list. Camacho y Orvañanos just happened to be the name of one of the biggest PR agencies in Mexico. When I walked in, to my wonder and disbelief, I was mistakenly identified as a professional model, and was sent on location to do a Corona Beer TV commercial. From then on, I continued to work on TV and as a model for companies like Catalina Bathing Suits, Orange Crush, Air France, etc.

But the original purpose of my trip was to learn Spanish at the Universidad Nacional Autonoma Mexicana. I had just finished my first year at UCLA, and was majoring in Spanish literature. When I arrived in Mexico, I was still filled with romantic images of Don Quixote fighting for his ideals and defending Dulcinea, his fair, albeit imaginary, maiden.

When I saw your father for the first time, surrounded by his friends on the college campus, I knew I had found my own living, breathing, Quixote! And it wasn't only because he was moving his hands in all directions, like a windmill, or even because he was tall, with long, skinny legs and lots of hair, it was because on the very day we met, he fought for my honor! Just like Don Quixote! (At least, that was the way I chose to see it.)

Toño was in his second-year of architectural studies. That day he and his friends had gone to Filosofia y Letras, (a special division of the University reserved for foreign students), to pick up American girls, like me, who came for the summer to study. In contrast to the proper, Mexican girls who needed chaperons, we American girls could go out alone. Since we had this freedom, we were judged as "easy", and sought out by the testosterone-laden young Mexican guys

That memorable day, I was having lunch at the school cafeteria of Filosofia y Letras. There was a young man sitting next to me who kept insisting that I let him take me home, and I kept answering in the negative. All of a sudden, apparently out of nowhere, the same tall, handsome student I had noticed earlier appeared, and forcefully told the insistent boy to "largarse" and leave me alone. When the boy stood firm, Toño and he agreed to settle their differences in the parking lot after school. Your dad won, fighting with his long, lanky legs and arms, and with more passion than style.

I know it is probably hard for you to imagine his being violent, but this was to be the first of many times that he "defended" me from the perceived windmills of other men's admiring stares and questionable intentions. And I'm sure it is no surprise to you that in the beginning, I was just as delirious, basking in the man who defended my honor.

Anyhow, when the fight was over, and with fresh blood on the green, tweed, sweater his sister had knitted for him, he triumphantly asked me in broken English "Ahora, now can I take you home?" And when I coyly hesitated, looked up at him, batted my eyelashes and answered in a barely audible, thin voice, "Well, I don't know," he answered with a very nonchalant, "If you say yes, that OK. If you say no, that OK, too. I no fight for you. I fight because I no like boys that bother pretty girls." I must admit, not quite the romantic or poetic Don Quixote response I had expected, but what the heck, you can't have everything!

Well, of course, he did take me home and we soon fell in love. Tall, dark and handsome, my Latin Don Quixote was only nineteen, but in my eyes he had no limits; no challenge was too great, no architect more talented, no businessman more visionary, no comedian funnier, and no boy more desirable than he. I compared him not only to the immature American boys back home, but also to his circle of Mexican friends, who followed him with what appeared to me, blind devotion. He was more charismatic, more charming, more confident, and cuter than any boy I had ever known. Starting to make sense?

Although we were in love, from the very beginning he swore he could never marry me because he had to marry someone Lebanese, preferably from Tabura, the village where his parents were from. But, one night, still fast asleep, I was awakened to the strings of violins and a tenor's voice. As you well know, being awakened by mariachis in the middle of the night is a traditional and cherished way for a man to show his love to a woman. But, I had never, ever heard of a serenade with violins and an opera singer! I ran to my window, which was on the third floor, praying, hoping, could it be? I excitedly opened the curtains, and there he was! My Don Quixote, your father, looking up to the apartment where I lived, accompanied by all of his faithful friends and more violin players than I could count. By his serenading me in that unique way, and with my father as a witness, I knew it was his way of proposing to me. As my teary-eyed father and I hugged each other, we both knew that soon I would be Mrs. Nacif, and become the first American-Jewish girl to marry a Mexican-Lebanese boy.

However, to make a future together a reality, and to be with your Dad, who was like a god to me, I would have to follow what I called your father's 10 Commandments.

1. Thou shalt wait five years
2. Thou shalt not date anyone else in those five years
3. Thou shalt not begin conversations, or have opinions, when thou interacts with men.
4. Thou shalt not look men in the eyes.
5. Thou shalt, no longer, wear heels with capris. In fact, thou shalt only wear skirts ... but not mini skirts.
6. Thou shalt only be allowed to have my sisters as your companions and friends.

7. *Thou shalt never go to a restaurant without me, or members of my family.*
8. *Thou shalt respect my parents, and call my mother every day.*
9. *Thou shalt not work once we are married.*
10. *Thou shalt be my queen, while I am the king who makes the rules.*

And, it goes without saying, I would have to stop doing the Corona beer commercials on TV, and modeling Catalina bathing suits, since these were disrespectful and unacceptable activities for a Lebanese wife. In his words, "Hay que sacrificar cinco años por una vida de amor y felicidad." ("We must sacrifice five years for a lifetime of happiness and love.")

All of the restrictions seemed unimportant in comparison with the family that I was to inherit. Nothing seemed hard. Nothing a sacrifice ... except for not being able to marry your father for over four years, and having to endure months and months of separation.

You see, Tono never lied to me. He even admitted he didn't think he was worth such a sacrifice, but that was the way things had to be so that I could fit in his world. He never pretended he could be, would be, or was remotely interested in interacting with me in the same way American men did with their wives, or that he believed in equality of the sexes.

Obviously, at that time in my life, equality wasn't important to me either. I wanted a man who had high morals and strict behavioral parameters. I wanted a man who was strong, confident, and knew who he was and what he wanted; a man I could follow. I wanted a man different from my father, who had always been unfaithful to my mother. In fact, when my father came to live with me in Mexico, your father taught him to respect me by forbidding him from bringing his dates to our house. It was young Antonio who made me feel secure and protected, and I loved him for that.

I believed that if Antonio prepared me and taught me, I could be a worthy Lebanese wife and mother. (No, not Mexican, because he and his family, as with all other ethnic groups in Mexico, held on to the culture and beliefs of their country of origin.) I admired who they were; a traditional, self-sacrificing family whose unconditional love for each other was timeless, and whenever I returned to Mexico, I felt like I was coming home.

So, four and a half years (and 785 letters) later, we married in the same Greek Orthodox Church where I had been, months earlier, baptized. The wearing of the crowns, the Bishop's long, sumptuous robes, the gold-engraved images, were difficult for my recently divorced, (and very Jewish), parents to accept, but to me, it was the happiest day of my life.

By the day of the wedding, I had won over the family with my sincere love for their son and my dedication to learn, not only the Arabic language, but the nuances of this very ritualistic culture. We didn't have any money of our own, so we lived with Toño's parents our first year. They cherished me, and made sure that everyone respected their little, blonde, American-Jewish daughter-in-law.

In hindsight, was it a mistake to give up a TV career, and my identity as an assertive American woman? We will never know, will we? What we do know is that I learned a loving way of being that I wouldn't have known otherwise, one that I have passed on to you and you will pass on to your own children. I gave you a father and a family who adore you and will always, always support you. And of course, it goes without saying, how could anything have been a mistake when the result of our love and innocence was the three of you?

When I got pregnant right away with you, Jenny, we were all beyond ourselves with joy. Your father went to a church that was in front of the clinic, knelt down, and with tears in his eyes, thanked God for his future child.

However, I was to discover later that everyone would have been a lot happier if you had been a boy, but you already know that. Up to then, I could deal with my own limitations, but my motherly instinct was already raging before you were born. You would not be treated as a less significant person because you were a girl!

When I was rolled into the spacious, private room at the American British Conway Hospital, (after giving birth to you, Jenny), I was amazed to find the room filled with so many people. Besides the family, there were dozens of my in-law's friends, all in black, standing in the waiting room. It felt more like a wake than a birth. Instead of the joyous tears and loving congratulations I expected, I saw only sad, resigned faces staring back at me. I was afraid something was dreadfully wrong. However, I was immediately assured you were perfectly healthy and very beautiful. But, to the chagrin of family and friends, you were born with a vagina instead of the preferred penis!

And, with a reassuring and comforting hug, my mother-in-law explained to me the rationale behind the forlorn countenances. "We love our daughter's as much as our sons. However, we cry when girls are born, because we know they come into the world to suffer."

And so was the resigned, albeit loving, reaction when Vivianne and Vannessa were born. Each time everyone tried to put on a "buena cara," but I knew they still believed it was my fault. (The fact the man's Y chromosome determined the sex of the child was just some propaganda invented by women.)

In fact, a plump woman with an accusing expression screamed at me when Vannessa was born. She waved her hands in the air and ranted, "Stupid, selfish girl, I told you that if you turned to the left after being intimate with Antonio, you would have a boy. You didn't do it, did you?"

Upon your birth, Jenny, the three of us left the protective arms and refuge of my in-laws, and we moved into our own place. That tiny, one bedroom apartment, with the turquoise round bed, surrounded by a matching organza tent, in the middle of the living room, symbolized for me the real beginning of our marriage. However, it was also the beginning of your father's fascination with playing cards at the Lebanese club, and at the same time, of many lonely nights for me.

The good news was that I was able to bring you up alone. While you absorbed the valuable Lebanese messages of respect for family, proper manners, and traditional priorities, I was able to read books to you about girls who could do, and be, anything they wanted. You learned that girls and boys were equal, as long as they were prepared equally for the world.

I know today that your father and his family are very proud of all of your accomplishments, but in those times, your ability to speak three languages before you were ten, your athletic achievements, and open personalities, were perceived as qualities that would chase possible marriage suitors away.

Over twenty years passed, and everyone saw us as the perfect family. We went through the stuff that life is made up of: illnesses, births, moves; along with the biggest earthquake ever known to Mexico; monetary devaluations that paralyzed the building of your father's hotel, and, even more importantly, my ability to buy clothes in the United States (just kidding!); nationalization of the banks and utilities; the death of beloved, bon vivant, Uncle Alfredo, and all the family meetings on how to financially and emotionally protect his seven children; weddings of most of your cousins; over fifty grandchildren and great grandchildren; Jenny and Vivi going away to school in the States.

On a personal level, I was dealing with the stress of constant loneliness, and trying to adapt to the limitations that I was warned of, but every day, the reminders of those limitations were more and more painful, and sapped my energy and joy. As I had been admonished, I couldn't have friends, go out to lunch with other women, sit in the same room with and share in the more interesting conversations of the men, or even go to the gym.

I am surprised, looking back on the many years I lived with an ever-increasing level of depression, that I did not get physically sick, since, according to Dr. Diane Schwartzbein, depression weakens the immune system, and is the leading cause of disability in women.

I was so busy with your everyday activities of ballet, drama, music, and language classes, as well as doctors and dentists, that I thought I was able to cover up, even from myself, how unhappy I was. Not surprisingly, one day I started to hyperventilate, and had a small breakdown, though I didn't know what it was at the time. I felt guilty, and pleaded with your father to forgive my constant tears and inability to get out of bed. Later, I would repeat to my audiences, "The lack of expression is always the cause of depression."

After two decades, we finally moved into the gorgeous house your father designed and built. There were four, expansive floors, flowing waterfalls, towering silk-leaf trees, an interior pool, a hand carved fireplace, and high wooden ceilings; a true tribute to your father's talent. However, it was never a home that reflected my choices or opinions, and I felt lonelier than ever.

Since Vivi and Jenny were already at universities in the States, I used the time to go back to school and get my masters degree in clinical psychology. And, although this new edifice was never a love nest, it was a perfect setting for me to begin, what would eventually become, my new career.

Every day for two years, large groups of women would come to my house to learn about new concepts; assertiveness, goal setting, self-esteem, and neuro-linguistics. Although I felt incongruent teaching what I didn't live, I was finding out that the skills I had intuitively used to help you to become the confident women you are today, also benefited the women that surrounded me.

The positive reaction I received from these eclectic groups of women gave me the courage to go against your father's rules and speak, eventually, at well-attended, (and well-remunerated), corporate meetings, often receiving standing ovations from the women in the audience! You, my darling Vivianne, would go to almost all of my key-note addresses. I will always remember your beaming face in the front row, as you enthusiastically and proudly clapped and sent me kisses.

Was it this newly acquired self-confidence that gave me the courage to leave my golden cage? Or was it the pain in my shoulders that eventually spread to my whole body, and partially paralyzed me? Sometimes, it's hard to know our true motivations why we do the things we need to do. But, I do know, five years ago I warned your father that if we didn't change the rules of our marriage, I would leave him. Five years was not a random number, but an exact calculation of when you, Vannessa would be off to college, and I would not bring shame to you or your sisters.

Well, the five years are up, and this time when we go to our summer-house in La Jolla, I will not be coming back to Mexico. I don't think your father really thought that I would leave. He had his own reasons for not wanting to address the reality of our situation, and I have to accept them. You girls, more than anyone, know that in his own way, he loved me, respected me, and always provided for us.

I know he feels I am a traitor to him and his love of twenty-five years, but all I can say is when I was eighteen, I made a promise that I couldn't keep. I believed in forever, and I believed even more in Toño.

Now, it's time for me to believe in myself; to live the freedom I gave you, and now yearn for myself; to be congruent with the messages of self-respect and self-determination I have taught you; to befriend my fear and know that she will inevitably be my constant companion in the beginning of this journey; to risk making mistakes, knowing that at least they will be my mistakes, and at the same time the only way I will ever learn to change and grow; and to, finally, discover who I am, and what I am capable of doing and becoming.

I cannot be any less than I have taught you to be!

I adore you, and promise to continue to make you proud of me,

su mami...

(February 1991)

Dearest Vannessa, Vivianne, and Jenny

It has already been six months since I left my family and life in Mexico. Can you believe it? I just realized that I was married and Mexican-Lebanese longer than I was American-Jewish. So, what does that say about me? I'll tell you. It says that at this moment I don't have a clue who I am.

As you know, during the first months I was elated with the reality of being free ... free to go anywhere and talk with anyone; free to take leisurely walks in the evening without being afraid; free to go to the gym and not be accused of flirting; free to go to the gym and flirt (if I wanted); free to drive my own car without a chauffeur; freedoms that everyone here takes for granted.

I race-walk at the cove every day, surrounded by the wildflower-covered rocks. When I take a water break, (or "hydrate" as people now say), I admire the seals as they play in the ocean and make their way up to the rocks to sunbathe. I watch the squirrels burrow and then stand at attention as they invariably out-stare me. Feeling my body move energetically and freely for the first time in almost three decades, I breathe deeply without feeling congested by smog. I feel happy. I feel at home.

I am forty-seven going on eighteen, because that was the age when the course of my life changed. Of course, nothing is the same. I'm not sure what I expected when I left Mexico, but not this. Often, I forget the names of the words in English, or don't understand the new colloquialisms. So many of the words are shortened, like condo for condominium, and they use "like" instead of "for example". I prefer to stutter than try to explain that I have forgotten my native tongue. I have this typical North American appearance on the outside, but on the inside I am still Lebanese.

What took me so long to learn; not looking men in the eyes, not permitting them to touch even my hand, not offering strong opinions, in other words, carrying myself in a certain way and being a proper and respectable Lebanese wife, are now habits that I have to unlearn. When I meet a man, I still immediately extend my hand to shake his and cast my eyes downward. Invariably I am left with my hand in the air looking for a place to go, and my eyes fixed on the floor. When I automatically attempt to give a woman a kiss on her cheek when we first meet, I quickly have to correct myself for fear she will think that I am getting too close and personal. But I am learning to follow the new rules. I hold myself back, just nod, and offer a cordial hello.

Speaking of kisses, you know how important, even sacred I consider them to be. They were always a symbol of love and possible commitment to us. Well, I might have to reconsider that belief also, since recently, a man invited me to "grow up" and become a part of the twentieth century. The challenge, my darlings, is looking deep into my being to discover what it is I truly believe, and what have I just unconsciously adopted as important. Once I can define what is mine ... own it ... know it to be true ... I will be able to live my truth with conviction.

I am discovering life is like every other learning process, in that we are never done. We must always be evaluating and reevaluating what we deem to be important. I guess everything has a price. I know I couldn't continue to live in a sheltered world where I didn't have permission to learn, grow, or make my own mistakes. Yet, at the same time, there is a part of me that misses the safety of my cushioned life, and I'm proud of the moral code I was taught, (and experienced), in Toño's world.

These unexpected feelings of ambivalence and not belonging are creating a lot of stress for me. And, since one of the main reasons I left Mexico was to be healthy and at peace, I have devised a sort of "recovery plan" for myself. Tell me what you think! Here it is.

Stay Connected
  A. Keep in touch with friends.
  B. Exercise
  C. Volunteer.
  D. Get a pet to love.
  E. Care about what's going on in the world.
  F. Take time to just be.
  G. Connect with my higher power through
     prayer and meditation.

And as I am following my coping plan, I will try to integrate the two worlds, without sacrificing my true essence. Not permitting passion to supersede heart, abandon to take priority over judgment, or delight to supersede self-respect will be my goals, in this, my new life. It seems that you, my three beautiful daughters, have already accomplished that goal, so as always, you will be my teachers and guides.

Oh yes, and I don't have the right clothes. I don't own any play clothes, and I'm not sure what to buy, since I can't afford a whole new wardrobe. I also need to change my hair. It's too stiff and formal. I need a cut that is more natural and flowing. Now, that is something I look forward to doing!

Yes, as we always say, life is an adventure. One can never look back. It would be like looking behind us with the side mirror on our car, and having it guide us to go forward. I can't look back, and must believe this decision is the best.

Les amo,
su mami

The What and How of Stress

Feeling angry, irritated, out of control, threatened and anxious, are words that people use to describe what they feel when they experience stress. We experience these feelings for different reasons, and what causes me to feel stressed is completely different than what provokes stress in someone else. The origin of the conflict or situation doesn't matter, but how we interpret it does.

Nothing means anything until we give it a meaning. That's worth repeating. It's not what happens, but the meaning we give to it, that causes us to react, positively or negatively. Some people become stressed when they have to give a speech others thrive on being in front of an audience. There are those who hate, even fear, novelty, newness, or traveling, while others need change to feel alive. A first date can be the cause of panic for some, and for others that first moment of contact is motive for anticipation and excitement.

Too much of a good thing can also cause stress, for our bodies prepare equally for a happy event, as they do for a dreaded or unhappy one. (I will have to leave the examples for your own definition of a joyful moment, since there are no universal positive or negative events. Even death can be considered positive in certain religions and under certain circumstances, while a birth, which for some mothers is the happiest day of their lives, can be experienced as negative if the child is unwanted, or the timing is bad.)

> The point is, your body doesn't know the difference between dis-stress (negative) and eu-stress (positive). All it knows is it has to get ready for an event that is out of the ordinary, so the adrenal glands send for extra amounts of adrenaline and cortisol to address the situation.

We are resilient, however a body that endures years of a constant state of stress feels threatened, and begins to lose its capacity to defend itself. Over time, the immune system fails, and illness, (including heart disease, cancer, and mental burnout), may result.

Let's take a look at what goes on in our bodies that causes stress and stress-related illnesses. An excess of cortisol, the stress hormone, creates havoc in our bodies. Nature had a very specific reason for creating cortisol. Many thousands of years ago, we lived in caves and had to deal with bears and saber-toothed tigers. When confronted by them, we had two options: fight or flee. Either fighting or fleeing took an extra boost of energy, so nature came up with a hormone that is secreted by the adrenal glands, called cortisol.

In this day and age, if we are properly socialized, we rarely fight or flee. Instead, we stay, we fume, and we grow resentful without saying anything. When this happens, cortisol accumulates in our bodies, and eventually harms every organ in our body, including our brains. It does this by robbing us of glucose, (the carbohydrate that fuels our brain), and by wreaking havoc on the neurotransmitters that send thoughts from one cell to the other.

It is very possible that what we thought of as inevitable aging is actually an accumulation of cortisol in our bodies. So, it goes to reason that the older we get, the more cortisol we have accumulated in the organs of our bodies.

At the same time, stress is a normal part of life. It's part of being alive! The goal is not a stress-free life, but a balanced one. The secret is to be aware when we feel overwhelmed and have tools to deal with acute and chronic stress. What we want to do is learn how to release bad stressors (distress) and not hold them in our brains and bodies.

Here are a list of stress symptoms. Some are inevitable, but if you have too many, then you are at a risk for illness (possibly in the coming year.) If you have more than three, be grateful that you are aware, and begin your stress reduction plan today.

Insomnia
Irritability
Anger
Restlessness
Nervous
Pain in shoulders
Tightness in the throat
Fatigue
Dry mouth
Fast or irregular heartbeat
Weight gain or loss
Difficulty concentrating or focusing
Depression
Melancholy
Nightmares

There are a number of steps we can take and tools we can use to decrease stress in our lives. Love, meditation, exercise, good nutrition, relaxation, and letting go of negative emotions, can all lower the level of cortisol, or as many call it, the death hormone, from our bodies. _(Other chapters in this book address in detail each of these stress-releasing antidotes, because in the same way they release stress, they are also anti-aging techniques.)_

During times of stress, our immune systems are especially

threatened, so it is important to protect them. The greatest enemies of cortisol are happiness and peace, and its best friends are toxic emotions, especially anger.

How Anger Harms Our Health

Anger not only eats away at our emotional well being, it also attacks almost every aspect of our physical health. According to Susan M. Lark, M.D., anger can cause and/or accelerate heart disease, high blood pressure, arthritis, inflammation, allergies, menstrual problems, and even excessive weight gain. In fact, several studies have linked anger to neck and back aches, muscle tension, and progression of coronary artherosclerosis. However, there are tools to release our lives of anger.

The most important rule when learning to deal with anger is to make a conscious effort to get rid of it. Although we might feel there is some temporary or long lasting gain in holding on to anger, that is NEVER the case.

If your anger is directed towards another person, here is an excellent exercise to do with him/her. Anger is like an onion. It has many layers, and fear is always at its core. The next time you are angry, sit down with your partner (friend, lover) and do this 5 step exercise.

1. I am angry, upset, furious, (use whatever word(s) fit for you) because: _____

2. I am hurt because: _____

3. I am afraid because: _____

4. I understand that: _____

5. I am grateful to you for: _____

6. And when the time comes, the most powerful antidote to anger are the words "I forgive you. I appreciate you," and "thank you."

However, if you have tried to explain, express yourself, understand, and forgive, and the result is only distress rather than happiness or pleasure, you must leave. In the beginning, it will be difficult, but eventually you will learn to only surround yourself with like-minded positive energy. The alternative will almost surely be depression.

Catching Depression in The Bud

Depression also causes large amounts of cortisol to be released into our bodies, so don't let yourself fall into depression! The longer we feel sad and depressed, the more cortisol we pump into our systems. And as you already know, cortisol can depress our immune system and lead to a myriad of illnesses, especially autoimmune diseases such as graves, rheumatoid arthritis, lupus, and multiple sclerosis.

Although depression is the natural response to loss, that dark cloud can also come on without our knowing the reason. The longer it lasts, the more difficult it is to overcome. I know this fact from my own experience with clinical depression. Here are some things we can do before we start the harmful cycle of taking anti-depressants.

Laughter: Studies have shown how laughter not only lightens our moods, but also sends a cascade of health-enhancing chemicals into our bodies. Often, just by going into a state of belly laughter, we can turn around our sad mood. Nothing can take the place of joy and laughter; not even good nutrition and exercise. Find out what makes you laugh. Look for the humor in the small stuff. I rent CDs of my favorite comedians and listen to them in the car, on the plane, and recently learned how to put them into my iPod. It's impossible to laugh and be depressed at the same time!

Self Love: While most men are "other" directed, and look to someone or something other than themselves to blame, women are "inner" directed, and tend to blame ourselves. Criticizing and putting ourselves down is so embedded in our minds that it's almost second nature. The secret is to change our nature!

Here is an exercise from the Institute of HeartMath in Boulder Creek, California:

1. Place your hand on your heart, close your eyes, and think of someone or something you love very much.

2. Just focus on that person or thing until the corners of your mouth begin to curl upward in a smile.

3. Notice that your heart rate has slowed, your muscles are no longer tense, and you have relaxed.

4. Tell yourself that you are to be counted as a loved one. Place yourself in the same scene in which you'd imagined the special person in step 2. Bask in the warm, relaxed glow of your heart's love, and say, "I am worthy." When you feel emotion welling up in your eyes, you'll know the message got in.

The Gift of Gratitude

When you express and experience feelings of gratitude and appreciation, your cardiovascular, immune, and hormonal systems are more likely to function at optimal levels. In a study from the Journal of Social and Clinical Psychology, volunteers were divided into three groups. Each of them was instructed to keep a daily log. The first group concentrated on five negative experiences, the second group wrote down five things they were better at than others, and the third group wrote five reasons to be grateful. At the end of three weeks, those who kept the gratitude journal reported increased energy, less health complaints, and greater feelings of overall wellbeing, as compared to the participants in the other two groups.

You can do the same. In her wonderful book, *"Simple Abundance"*, by Sarah Ban Breathnack, the author suggests keeping a gratitude journal. She recommends that each day you write down at least 5 new reasons to be grateful. Imagine going through life focusing on reasons to be appreciative! And what about looking for five new reasons every day to be grateful for your partner, children or friends?

Oprah Winfrey said this book changed her life by making her look for, and magnify, the good in her life. And yes, try being grateful and stressed at the same time. I dare you!

There is also a technique to relieve stress that is very old, and beginning to be practiced in the United States, called autogenic training, created by a German neurologist, Johannes Shultz. This procedure involves repeating a series of pre-determined phrases, thereby inducing a meditative state of complete relaxation. This technique can restore mental equilibrium, enhance coping skills, relieve panic attacks, chronic pain, and overcome insomnia. I think it is worth the time to go over the easy steps that will help you relax, and build up your nervous and immunological system.

Basic training starts with six simple phrases that must be practiced repeatedly, in sequence. The seventh phrase is one that you devise yourself to meet your needs. This is also an ideal technique to do a few weeks before an operation or taking a test. The seventh statement would be: "I will be relaxed and open to healing my body." Or, "I am calm and confident, because I am prepared."

Sit in a chair or lie down, close your eyes, and silently repeat the following 6 phrases, in order, for up to 15 minutes, 3 times a day.

   1. My body is heavy.

   2. I am very warm.

   3. My heartbeat is calm and regular.

   4. My breathing is calm and regular.

   5. My abdomen is warm and relaxed.

   6. My forehead is cool and clear.

   7. Your unique statement; for example,
   "I will sleep well the entire night."

To end the session, close your eyes and take deep breaths, make a fist with each hand, and bend your arms toward your chest.

Words Are More Than Syllables

What we say to ourselves, in the privacy of our own thoughts, has a profound effect on how we feel and what we do. Somehow we have the magical thinking that if no one else knows about our negative self talk, it won't harm us (or them.) Nothing could be further from the truth. Have you ever been muscle tested? A health practitioner asks you to hold one hand out, while she repeats certain words or affirmations. With positive ones, such as "I am strong" it is almost impossible for her to budge your arm. A negative affirmation such as "I am ashamed and weak" results in a limp arm that is easily pushed down. Although I never understood the reason, I have been aware of this phenomenon for years. However, I recently read a book, titled "The Hidden Messages in Water", by Masaru Emoto, wherein he provides an explanation of how and why words have such a profound effect on our health.

If you saw the movie, "What The Bleep Do We Know?!", I am sure you were impacted when you saw with your own eyes how Dr. Emoto's experiments proved that even water is effected by thought and words. When exposed to words like "thank you", "love", and "gratitude", the water consistently formed beautiful crystals. While words like "Satan", or "You Fool", formed completely different crystals. What is the explanation to this scientific research? In Dr. Emoto's words: "Water-so sensitive to the unique frequencies being emitted by the world ... mirrors the outside world ... (It) faithfully mirrors all the vibrations created in the world, and changes these vibrations into a form that can be seen with the human eye. When water is shown a written word, it receives it as a vibration, and expresses the message in a specific form". If your thoughts were converted into a form, what would it look like? What color would it be?

Not only do our thoughts have a direct effect on our health, but, what we send out into the world is what we will be drawn to us. We cannot receive what is fundamentally different from us. In other words, if we want to attract love, prosperity, peace, and joy in our lives, we must send love, prosperity, peace, and joy into the world.

Simple Remedies with Powerful Results

There is nothing more blissful than taking a relaxing bath with essential oils, such as chamomile or lavender. For menopausal stress, yarrow is wonderful because this essential oil relieves tension in the pelvic area. Breathing in an essential oil such as lavender or ylang ylang can alter our brain's neuro-chemistry as they increase the alpha brain waves associated with relaxation. Even something as simple as yawning can help to release stress by stretching the muscles, increasing oxygen intake, and releasing tension. Yawn loudly and stretch your arms several times a day. Try snacking on nuts, because they have lots of magnesium and B-vitamins, which relax you and help concentration.

As always, I recommend vitamins, minerals and herbs, because it is almost impossible to get what we need from food sources. Take vitamins B-complex vitamins, magnesium, and calcium; herbs such as kava and ginseng toot, gotu kola have been used for centuries to combat anxiety and fatigue.

> **Remember, it's not what happens to you (stressors) that has the potential to kill you. It's the meanings that we give to words and events, and how we respond to them, that put us in harm's way.**

If we choose to give positive meanings to the events that occur in our lives, we will experience very little stress. For example, instead of seeing my marriage as a failure, and myself as a victim, I can choose to take responsibility for my choice, and congratulate myself for moving into a healthier and more joyful stage of my life. We all have options, and I call them Cortisol Busters. We have mentioned some, but they're worth repeating!

Cortisol Busters

Exercise! This was the way nature meant for you to deal with stress.

Live in the Here and Now.

Lose yourself in something that you love.

Become a child again.

Belly laugh.

Forgive.

Meditate.

Detoxify.

Breath Deeply.

Practice yoga.

Enjoy aromatherapy

Let go of whatever you are holding onto by writing, talking, or praying.

Verbally vent (preferably by yourself).

State your needs in a respectful way using "I statements." For example, "I get very upset when you come home late and need for you to call me."

Cry.

Hit a pillow.

Decide to change the things you can, accept the things you can't, and ask God to give you the wisdom to know the difference.

Surround yourself with friends and family.

Release your control to a higher power.

Learn to say "no" without feeling guilty.

Love your work.

Leave your work at work.

Dance (even if it's with yourself).

Write a grateful journal.

Smile.

Focus on others instead of yourself.

Cortisol Busters (continued)

> Touch and be touched (even if it's with yourself).
> Get a massage.
> Look for the positive meaning, even in difficult moments.
> Find the success in your failure.
> Have sex as often as you can! (Even if it's with yourself.)
> Let optimism, not fear, rule your reason.
> List and prioritize your goals.
> Keep high (but realistic) expectations.
> Give yourself one special experience or present a day.
> Spend time in nature, and away from technology.
> Above all, love and receive love.

Only you know what makes time stand still for you. Only you know what words you can say to yourself that make you feel better. Only you have the answers. Since we are all different, I invite you to make your own list of what keeps you in the present, and calms you down. Maybe fishing? Bowling? Watching reality television? Reading? Gardening?

> **Listen to yourself, love yourself, take the time to take care of you. So few things are worth making ourselves sick over, and we invent most of them.**

Catch yourself saying negative comments about you or others, and change them for compassionate and forgiving ones. Monitor your breathing, and if it is shallow, take a few deep breaths. Notice when you feel tense and learn to relax each and every part of your body. Open your heart to all of your blessings and be so very grateful. As Miguel Ruiz says in, "The Four Agreements", don't take anything personally. It is never about you. He also says not to assume. I say, never assume the worst.

"The afternoon of human life
must also have a significance of its own
and cannot be merely a pitiful appendage
to life's morning."

~ Carl Jung

Chapter Four

Spirituality

(1985)

On Jenny's graduation from high school in Mexico City.

Dearest Jenny,

You did it, my darling!!! You never had any doubts. You not only graduated, but as president of your class, you handed out the diplomas to 1,700 of your peers at the American School. I sat there with your father and grandfather, who had flown in to witness this remarkable occasion that we were told would never happen. We sat so straight, stretching our necks, so as not to miss one moment.

Once again you have shown your teachers ... you've proven against all the statistics ... confirmed that doctors, no matter how famous, don't always have the last word, and demonstrated that the human spirit, with its miraculous, incomprehensible strength is able to heal and create miracles.

You were only twelve, and I will never forget sitting next to you while we watched your older cousin receive her diploma from the class president. Your eyes were fixed on the young woman who was handing out the diplomas. Even though we didn't know the outcome of the new meds, you whispered to me that you would be the one handing out the diplomas when you graduated from high school. I smiled, humoring you, knowing that we would be lucky if you could even stay in school.

At that time, your hair was kinky because of the reaction to the anti convulsive drugs, you tired easily, and worst of all, you could only learn auditorily. In other words, your mind couldn't absorb the words on the page through your eyes. You had to hear them with your ears. In order for you to pass your classes I had to read the text to you and your teachers agreed to give you the tests orally. So you see, my love, just getting a passing grade was an amazing feat. You were already my hero, just because you never gave up. But, being elected class President was something that I could never have dreamed of. How did you know that you could do anything to which you set your mind?

Was it only four years ago that I received a phone call from the neurologist who so coldly and matter-of-factly left me the message on my answering machine that would change our lives forever? "Señora Nacif, Jennifer tiene un tumor en el cerebro, por eso ha estado vomitando. Su enfermedad se llama epilepsia abdominal." ("Mrs. Nacif, Jennifer has a brain tumor, and that is the reason for her obsessive vomiting. Her condition is called abdominal epilepsy.")

A brain tumor? How does a mother let those words seek into her mind? How could that be? Your only symptom was throwing up and then falling asleep for hours and hours. I had never heard of abdominal epilepsy, and apparently I wasn't alone. I just thought you were going through some strange premenstrual phase.

Our search to find the best doctor and correct medication for you took us to Beverly Hills, California, where we were told you would need brain surgery! With tears in his eyes, my father stood and trembled as he waited outside of the doctor's office, offering to pay for the surgery we couldn't afford. But, we weren't satisfied with the prognosis, and continued our search in Mexico.

So many doctors, so many dead ends, so many contradictory opinions, so many different medications! But you never complained. You never accepted that you were limited. We finally returned to our beloved family doctor, who tweaked your medicines, so that you could have a normal life, though he admonished you not to ride a bike or do sports. Of course you didn't listen, and were captain of the volleyball team!

Did you always know that everything would work out for the best, and your illness could not keep you from becoming the strong, capable, and determined woman you are today? What did you know that none of us, not even the doctors, didn't know?

And now, my lovely Jenny, you are off to Poughkeepsie, New York. Marist College has a special program where you will be tutored privately, and learn by hearing books on cassettes. As we have analyzed together, you will be entering a new environment; in comparison to the warm and nurturing climate and temperament of your Mexican world, you will have to adapt to chilly surroundings. But you're not afraid; not because you are unaware or naive, but because, as you've told me many times, "new experiences don't scare me; they excite me."

You held fast to your vision of living life fully, and defied everyone when they predicted your physical and mental limitations; the teachers, the statistics, even the world-renowned specialists. I have no doubt this passion and tenacity will always be your guiding light in life. Knowing our purpose, and then letting it direct our choices is the secret to a worthwhile life. You are so young, yet you seem to already be guided by an inner purpose.

I want to tell you a story about two, grown women who never knew their inner purpose, and for that reason, their lives ended prematurely.

I was fourteen or fifteen, and felt like a grown up in the black sequin dress with a low neck that my mother bought for me for this occasion. It was my very first slinky dress, though all the padding in the world couldn't give cleavage to my flat chest. It was 1959, and the Golden Globe Awards, the foreign press' equivalent of the Oscars, was being celebrated in the banquet room of our local Racquet Club.

If it was the pompous occasion that it is today, I wasn't aware. All of my attention was focused on the much older, handsome, blond, and very tan tennis teacher that shared the table with us. (I was positive he was flirting with me.) I was oblivious to the celebrities that came to the table, to give exaggerated hugs and "double-cheek" kisses to our friend, Judy, from the Israeli press. Actually, I was more concerned that my foam rubber falsies might fall into my salad, and the tennis teacher would know I was not really well endowed.

However, later in the evening, when I was coming out of the bathroom, right in front of me were Marilyn Monroe and Judy Garland. Can you imagine that? It was one of those moments that you never forget. They were both so beautiful; Judy in a bright red, long gown, Marilyn in a black, tight, sequined dress, and yes, she certainly filled it out with her perfect curves, and very enviable bust.

But it wasn't only their fame or beauty that made this an unforgettable moment. Judy Garland was holding Marilyn Monroe strongly with both hands tightly interlocked at her elbows, and looking firmly and intensely in her eyes. I heard her clearly and vehemently say: "Be Happy! Be Happy! That's all that matters," and then she hugged her. I think it was the last appearance for both before their deaths. Judy Garland knew that more important than fame, more important than beauty, more important than anything, was what to them had been unattainable ... happiness.

What a great and sad story, no?
Judy Garland and Marilyn Monroe
got lost in the maze of other people's
demands. Too late, they realized that
guarding and creating their own happiness was
the real work of life.

We are all pilgrims, forging our ways through our lives.
Some, like you, Jenny, are in the first act, and some, like me,
are in the third. We fight the dragons when necessary, and
learn to hold on to ourselves and to our visions.

As always, you are teaching me to be brave. I'll remember
your courageous words and positive attitude when I am
missing you, and tempted to ask you to return to the
security of my arms. And I'll tell myself that I have nothing
to worry about, because my Jenny, (as you proved today),
can do anything she sets her mind to.

Dearest indomitable daughter, as you leave me, please
continue to make knowing yourself a practice. I know you
will be busy, and it might seem inconsequential to sit down
and quietly reflect, or meditate, on the beauty of nature and
the power of the universe. Find that still place of joy within
you that remains uncorrupted by the static of everyday life.

As I remember how you triumphed over so many

"insurmountable" obstacles, I am filled with joy and inspiration. You continue to teach me and give me strength, Jenny, in watching you, I know that wisdom has nothing to do with age, and everything to do with believing in yourself.

I love you,
tu mami

Author's Note: Today, my Jenny is the mother of two beautiful little girls, and is a well known and beloved television personality. She continues to stand out from the rest by being an example for self determination and family values. She lovingly endured an under water birth which was watched on television by thousands of her admirers, and is an advocate for breast feeding, which she enjoyed more than two years. Jenny has written a highly acclaimed book called "Los Cuatro Idiomas del Amor", (The Four Languages of Love), and has her own product line called "Scentual Potions." She has permitted me to share her secret, with the hopes that other young girls will know that nothing is impossible, if you believe in yourself!

The What and How of Spirituality

Creating a habit or a practice that stills your mind and allows you to connect with something greater than yourself not only can give you inner peace, but also can prolong your life and enhance your health.

According to Rabbi Shoni Labowitz, in her teachings of the Kabbalah, (Jewish mystical teachings), before we can go within and find our source, we must empty. As it is impossible to think clearly when we are overwhelmed, or eat when we are stuffed, or process when we are filled with too much data, it is impossible to settle down when our minds are filled with clutter, such as expectations, thoughts, and stimulation.

It is only when our cup is empty that we can fill it. As the analogy of the Zen practice teaches us, if you present a full rice bowl to the universe, it cannot be filled; if you present an empty rice bowl, the universe will fill it. "Let go, release, relinquish, and stand ready to be filled by the Infinite Source."

> In the chaos and business of everyday life, we can quickly crowd our minds with tasks, details, worries, and noise. Yet, we know we are spiritual beings, that there is something more than money, power, looks, or knowledge. We know the origins of love, intuition, hope, and peace all come from a higher power.

When that inner voice calls to you to be quiet, how do you answer? Have there been times when you have emptied and prepared yourself to receive the true you? Right now, stop what you are doing. Take a deep breath and calm your mind. Empty.

Open. Release. Do this three times. Do you feel more serene? You can do this anytime; when you are fearful, when you are hurried, when you are overwhelmed in thought. It takes time, but I promise you, you will begin to get closer to your higher self and your divine nature.

There are so many ways to enter into stillness and connect with our source! Regardless of how you choose to create your spiritual practice, you will find that once you do, joy and intuition are closer to you than ever before. Many times, people realize the solutions to urgent problems or long unanswered questions during meditation.

Here are five powerful approaches to spiritual practice:

Meditation

For thousands of years, monks throughout the world have sat in contemplative silence, meditating as part of their path to enlightenment. But research shows that you don't have to be a monk ... or spend your life meditating ... to enjoy meditation's benefits.

Meditation is the process of gradually stilling the body and the breath, so you can focus on a spiritual center or source. Meditation is not a religion in and of itself; it is just a way to help your muscles and your mind become calm and focused.

Meditation on Breath
Pause a moment and sit comfortably in a chair or on the floor. As you slowly inhale and exhale, feel the breath moving into your body. Allow your inhaling and exhaling to flow evenly and freely. In the quiet stillness, begin hearing the sound of the breath, and know that it is the

breath of God as it enters your body. Slowly inhale and feel the breath of God entering through the top of your head and moving through your entire body. Now see the breath of God as it flows through your entire image. Hear, feel, and see the breath until the sound, sense, and sight of it become one in your body...Pause. Relax and luxuriate in the breath, the calm, the stillness, the peace.

In the beginning, it doesn't matter how long you meditate, where you meditate, or in what position. All that matters is that you do it consistently! Once I get out of the habit, it is a challenge to begin again. I ask myself, "Why? Why don't I meditate more often, since I know how wonderful I feel after I meditate? I know that my day goes better, that everything looks brighter, better, newer, happier." But somehow, it seems that other activities are more important, like cleaning drawers, making phone calls, or just about anything.

When I comment on this reluctance to meditate, here are other excuses I hear from my friends, and the answers that I give them.

"I Can't Keep My Mind Still"
Of course you can't. That's just the way our minds work.

What to do: Just listen to your breath, or repeat a word or phrase like, peace, or love, or one.

"I Can't Sit Still That Long"
Ditto. Your body and your mind want to move.

What to do: When you get the urge to move, give it a positive meaning. Tell yourself that you are beginning to encounter what every meditator must ... the temptation to get up. Repeat, "Stay, stay," and go back to listening to your breath. Or, you can practice walking meditation. Walk slowly and breathe at the same rhythm as your steps. With your eyes lowered, notice the contact of your feet with the ground, and continue to focus on your breath and on walking.

"I Fall Asleep"
Once again, since we are relaxed, it is a message to our brains to go to sleep.

What to do: Try sitting straight, with your spine erect and your feet firmly planted on the ground. You can keep your eyes open, or bring them up to the center of your eyebrows.

"It Makes My Back (Neck, rear end, etc.) Hurt"
See if it's just restlessness. If so, stay with it. It's really hard just to stay still. If sitting is too painful, lie down or try walking. Open your eyes and focus on something specific a few feet in front of you. If you continue to fall asleep, let yourself. You probably are sleep deprived.

"I Don't Have Time"
You may not think meditating is that important, or may be afraid you won't be able to, and use this as an excuse. All you need is ten minutes a day. We all have that.

What to do: Make a specific time everyday. Begin with ten minutes and build up to more later. We can all get up ten minutes earlier, or watch less TV before going to sleep. We are so used to working hard, it's difficult to fathom how just being at peace can have so many benefits.

"I Don't Do It Right"
There is no right or wrong way. Whatever works for you,

do it. We need to take it out of the esoteric realm and know it is not just for Buddhist monks.

"I Don't Notice Anything"
You might not feel a change to begin with.

What to do: Have no expectations. Trust, (as you do when you lift weights or exercise), that in the long run this will be very good for you. Just be patient, and you will see that the calm you feel will seep into your everyday experiences. You eventually will feel more balanced, less stressed, and at peace.

In 20-Minute Retreats, Rachel Harris, Ph.D., suggests mini retreats that are divided into three parts. First, find a comfortable spot and make sure pencil and paper are ready. Now, close your eyes and focus on your breathing for four minutes. Your body will relax little by little. Second, open your eyes and spend about three minutes with pen and paper in hand, and answer the following questions: What do you need—not want—to do for yourself now? What is most important to you in your relationships with friends, partner, and family? What is your spiritual intention for the rest of your day?

Reread what you wrote before you go to sleep, and let your unconscious deliver to you what you have requested.

Prayer

When you believe that God is a presence in your life, then you may choose to schedule a time each day, or twice a day, to immerse yourself in prayer. Conversation with God takes you away from the frustrations of your life, and allows you to hand those worries over to a higher power. Prayer is positive energy, and can come in the recitation of the rosary, in your own words, in the silence of meditation, and in any other ways where you are open to receive the inner light of God.

Many fears have been calmed through prayer. Often, people find that a combination of prayer and meditation is the most effective, spiritual practice for them. When prayer comes from a place of acceptance ... not demanding ... and emanates from the infinite light, anything can be overcome. The Kabbalah says the inner light of God is kindled and rekindled in you with the assistance of prayer.

In his book, *"Prayers, A Communion with our Creator"*, Don Miguel Ruiz says, "In prayer, we quiet all the voices talking inside our heads that tell us why something isn't possible, and open a direct channel to our faith. When we pray we use the voice of the human, but we align with the voice of our hearts, our spirits, (to achieve our intention), and that is what makes the prayer powerful."

A prayer from Don Miguel Ruiz:

"Today, Creator, I ask you to open my eyes and open my heart so that I can recover the truth about my life...

Today, Creator, let me see what is, not what I want to see. Let me hear what is, not what I want to hear. Help me to recover my awareness so that I can see you in everything I perceive with my eyes, with my ears, with all my senses.

Let me perceive with eyes of love so that I find you wherever I go and see you in everything you create.

Help me to see you in every cell of my body, in every emotion of my mind, in every person I meet.

Let me see you in the rain, in the flowers, in the water, in the fire, in the animals, and in the butterflies.

You are everywhere, and I am one with you. Let me be aware of this truth.

And, I want to share with you a prayer that was written for me by Ayleyaell, a woman filled with grace, who was sent to me by a miracle when I needed her most.

Unfailing Radiant Light of Source,
I AM calling your profound grace into my life now. (3X)

Unfailing Radiant Light of Source,
I AM calling your profound perfection into my relationships now. (3X)

Unfailing Radiant Light of Source,
I AM calling deep peace and compassion to embrace
All action on Earth Mother now.

Therefore, I ask all discordant energy, all anxieties and stress, be now dissolved and transmuted into Light, Quiet, Illumination, and
Love Divined forevermore.
I ask and accept deep peace and rest, moving
Unto and into me,
Melting all human tension
Into the sweetness
And the delight of Spirit's Unfailing Love Eternal. (3X)"

Resources
The Power of Positive Thinking, **Norman Vincent Peal** gives anecdotal evidence of the power of prayer to positively change lives.

There's a Spiritual Answer to Every Question, **Wayne Dyer** emphasizes the power of prayer as a way to influence one's joy of life, concerns, and sense of connectedness to God.

In the Sanctuary of the Soul, A Guide to Effective Prayer, **Paramahansa Yogananda** explains the attitudes and approaches to talking with God that reap the greatest results for the person praying.

Miraculous Living, **Rabbi Shoni Labowitz** combines the Talmud with ancient Asian disciplines.

Yoga

All of a sudden it seems everyone is practicing this ancient and timeless art, science, and philosophy. There are now over 16 million practitioners in the U.S., according to a Yoga Journal estimate. The reason for its popularity is, once you begin, you can't live without doing your "asanas" (positions). Yoga provides so many benefits; it's hard to count them all! It makes you feel strong, clears your mind, makes you flexible, and above all ... brings you peace. You won't get any of those benefits in a spinning, or step class.

It took me a long time to even try it because I have been so much into physical and strenuous exercise. Then, when I took my first class, I compared myself to everyone else, and not being able to balance on one leg or touch my toes with my head, discouraged me, and it took me ten years to begin again. Now, I do IYengar yoga twice a week.

Contrary to what I thought, you don't have to be elastic to practice yoga. In fact, part of the beauty of yoga is starting exactly where you're at, and feeling the changes that occur little by little. If that means you can't touch your toes, so be it. If it means you can barely bend at your waist, that's fine too. The secret is to go to the edge, but not to strain. There is a fine line that only you know.

Listening deeply to your body's truth, which is whatever you're experiencing in the moment, and honoring that experience by pulling back if necessary, is one of yoga's most important lessons. Those of us who grew up hearing "no pain, no gain" need to change our mantra, because in the yoga studio, pain generally means no gain.

But, that doesn't mean it's easy. Often your muscles will ache, because holding many of the poses are challenging. I still lose balance, stick my rear end out too far, and bend my legs. However, now I know that all of these limiting experiences are part of the practice. It's about being vigilant of what is going on in your body, and maintaining your equanimity, even when experiencing a difficult or challenging sensation. Many of the ways I react to my limitations in yoga are how I react when I leave the yoga studio.

As I mentioned before, I do Iyengar Yoga. I chose this form, originally, because I saw the dramatic changes in my daughter's posture and flexibility, and I fell in love with her strict and dynamic teacher, Sue, in Los Angeles. Iyengar yoga, created by B.T.S Iyengar, is characterized by great attention to detail, and precise focus on body alignment. Iyengar pioneered the use of "props" such as cushions, benches, blocks, straps, and even sand bags, which function as aids allowing beginners, like myself, to perform the asanas, that otherwise I probably couldn't do. This way I get the benefit of years of practice, although I am a beginner.

There are almost as many variations on yoga as there are teachers.

Hatha yoga, the most popular style, combines meditation, physical poses, and breathing techniques to harmonize the mind, body, and spirit. Other styles, like Bikram (also known as hot yoga, because the room is heated) or Astanga (Power Yoga), can help you recover from injury, manage your weight, and strengthen your immune system, but they can also push your limits, so be ready to sweat. Kundalini yoga includes chanting and visualization. A wide range of other styles and poses can help with everything from chronic pain to frustration. And anytime you're feeling overwhelmed in a class, it's okay to go into child's pose and rest.

Art

The artists among us often find that in the act of creating music, paintings, poetry, or dance, they connect with something greater. Losing yourself in an artistic practice on a regular basis is like yoga, in that it brings you naturally into the rhythm of the life force around and within you.

Art can also be used as therapy, for it permits us to express our emotions in a nonthreatening way, by drawing on our nonlinear part of the brain. We don't have to be talented to express inner conflict through dance, drama, sculpting, or music. All of these disciplines promote concentration, imagination, and creativity as colors, sounds, and movements create order and form for both the mind and body. There isn't a right way or a wrong way to express our creativity, and sometimes it's the only way.

Nature

For some people, there can be no greater transcendental experience than observing the beauty in nature. Taking an hour a day to be among the Fall leaves, lapping waves, mountains, or near horses or other pets, can free your mind and body from worries and cares. Finding a beautiful place to pray, meditate, practice yoga, or create your art enhances and heightens these other spiritual experiences.

"Pause, empty, and listen to the sounds of the wind, the melody of your soul, the heart of the one you love. Stop a moment and smell the leaves of the trees, the mist of the ocean, the fragrance of the air. Slowly open your eyes to the beauty that surrounds you and mirrors God" (*Miraculous Living*, by Rabbi Shoni Labowitz).

Inspirational Thoughts

"The dark night of the soul comes just before revelation.
When everything is lost, and all
seems darkness, then comes the new life and
all that is needed."
~ Joseph Campbell

The one who is attached to things will suffer much.
The one who saves will suffer heavy loss.
A contented human is never disappointed.
The one who knows when to stop
never finds himself or herself in trouble.
He or she will stay forever safe.
~ Lao Tzu

"To lengthen thy life,
lessen thy meals."

~ Benjamin Franklin

Chapter Five

Nutrition

(1983)

Dear Vivi and Vannessa,

You don't have to stay. I know this hasn't been the experience I promised you. I had so hoped you would be happy in the United States. I wanted you to learn about, and be proud of all your heritages: Mexican, Jewish, Lebanese, and now, North-American.

By going to school here for a year, I had hoped you would understand why I am so proud to have been born in the United States. My head was filled with visions and my heart with hope and excitement. You would be free; free to ride your bikes, to play outside with your new friends, to build sand castles, to swim at the beach, and to attend public school ... things you couldn't do in Mexico for all the reasons you know. How we looked forward to going to the supermarket and buying all the cookies, candy, and junk food we couldn't get in Mexico! I could just see you jumping up and down as your eyes took in all the yummy choices of the supermarket. I especially envisioned your speaking English with all of your new friends, and sharing with them stories about your life in Mexico.

But it hasn't turned out the way I hoped, or we thought it would.

I wouldn't blame you if you wanted to go home where you are accepted, happy, and comfortable. You both have done your best, and it hurts me to see you so unhappy. You can return to your school and your friends in Mexico. I have arranged it with the principal.

Let me tell you I am so proud of the way you have handled yourselves these past months. And at the same time, I am really sorry for bringing you into a world that has changed so much from when I lived here. Or maybe it hasn't. I just wasn't aware! Vivi, it wasn't your fault. When you were asked to write a composition entitled "The Person Who Has Sacrificed the Most in History," you chose me. Thank you, my sweet daughter. Your teacher was amazed at your perfect English as you read your essay out loud.

Your new classmates weren't expecting an answer like the one you gave, because they chose people from the history book you have been reading. And at the same time, they take for granted that their moms do the things that you think are so wonderful.

"I chose my mommy because she has to get up early, make our breakfast, take us to school, and help us with homework. She is sacrificing herself for us because she wants us to know our American culture. At home in Mexico, we have maids and a chauffeur that get up with us and take us to school, so my mommy can wait up for our Daddy and go to sleep late. Now, she's alone and misses him so much, and he's home with our maids, Laya and Marsela and our chauffeur, Victor."

When you visit your friend's homes, you will notice they do the chores by themselves or, ideally, help each other. And just as their mothers and dads do special things for them out of love, so do I. It is no sacrifice, my love.

When you came home crying and asked me why the children made fun of you and called you a "beaner" and a "wet back",

I was shocked and at a loss for words. All I could do was hold you in my arms. It was your first experience with prejudice ... and amazingly, mine, too.

Though I am not defending ignorance or cruelty, sometimes, when people don't understand something, or when it doesn't fit into what they have been told, or when it is just different, they can become mean and unfair. I don't understand it either. But they just don't get how much it hurts when they call people names or make fun of them.

It's really important that you forgive them, not so much for them, but for you. Holding on to anger or resentment hurts us, and in the long run, harms our spirits and our health.

Vannessa, all of a sudden you, too, entered a world where you were treated like less ... a world where being Mexican and having beautiful brown hair and eyes was not considered beautiful. The blue-eyed, blonde-haired girls (that you tell me are called "bops") have excluded you from their elite "popular" world, and you have felt so confused and lonely. I understand that feeling. Feeling like an outsider is not reserved only for beautiful little girls like you who were born in Mexico.

When I was fifteen, and in the tenth grade, I wanted to be accepted as a member of the Lorelles, the most popular club in my high school. I guess you could say they were like the "bops" in your school. In those days we weren't judged by our ethnicity, but by the name of the club we put on the binder of our notebooks. Being a Lorelle meant you were "in", "cool", popular. Sans Parelles were the smart girls, etc.

As we walked down the crowded halls of Hamilton High, we were stereotyped depending on the name of the club we associated with. But, the worst thing that could possibly happen to any girl, was to have no name written on her notebook, because that meant that no one wanted her. So, I dreamed of putting the name "Lorelle" in large letters on my notebook, because it meant automatic acceptance and approval. I fantasized walking along the school's hallways with my head high in the air and being recognized as a member of the popular group.

But in order to be voted into the prestigious club, you had to go to different events, such as buddy days and teas, after which the members would vote you in or out. Three black balls (meaning three girls that didn't like you) were enough for you to be excluded from a "life" of fun and dates. Going to the obligatory buddy days and teas, where the members closely scrutinized how you dressed and talked, I tried hard to fit in and have everyone like me. Yet, on the day of the voting, as I anxiously awaited the treasured phone call of acceptance, there was never a ring. Well, that isn't completely the truth. My phone did ring six times: my six best girl friends were on the other line screaming with happiness because they had been accepted into the exclusive circle of Lorelle's. Of my six best friends, I was the only one who didn't receive the treasured and awaited acceptance phone call.

I never understood why I was the only one who was rejected. I never knew why my notebook would always remain empty and I would never be seen as someone who was worthy or deserving of popularity. I felt like there must be something wrong with me, and it took me many, many years to get over this unconscious feeling of being less, and to finally realize that it wasn't about me at all, but about them. (Many years later I was told I was ostracized because I was too emotional and moved my hands too much.)

Judging someone because of a name on a notebook is as ridiculous as judging someone because of the color of their skin, or eyes, or hair. I pray it won't take you years to realize that your worth emanates from your heart and your good deeds. The opinions of others are just that; opinions. And the only opinion that counts about you is yours!!

I am reading this letter to you out loud, because I want to make sure we can always talk about the stuff that hurts. Sometimes it just stays inside and feels like a hole in our stomachs. Giving these feelings words can free us to be our loving selves again.

I truly believe that everything, especially the hard stuff, is an opportunity for us to share and get closer and closer. I know it's hard to believe, but everything that seems "bad," darlings, is not always bad at all. Being uncomfortable and awkward are signs that something new is about to happen. If we didn't let ourselves feel "icky," we would just be doing the same stuff all the time and would never discover new and wonderful things.

For instance, look at me cooking healthy meals. Until we came here and I took the course on nutrition, I didn't know that all those crispy, salty potato chips, sweet cake mixes with their frostings, and yummy Twinkies, and Ding Dongs were so bad for you. I didn't know that cooking with so much oil when I made dishes like pork chops in coke and fried platano machos could one day make us really sick.

Now, every day, I learn a little bit more about how to buy the right kinds of foods: green vegetables, proteins like fish and nuts, and really good fruits like mangos, blueberries, papayas, and apples. I love learning how to prepare healthy food for you as a new way of expressing my love. It's not a sacrifice, although sometimes you have to endure my dry or burnt experiments. But when I prepare a healthy,

delicious meal for us,
I do a little dance
inside. Who is this
woman who can take on
the delicate balance of her own
body and do it so deliciously? It's me!

Anyone for trout almandine with crisped greens and wild rice pilaf? How about salmon ravioli or egg-white quiche? Well, at least I'm not making you drink that disgusting, diluted liver drink I read about in an Adele Davis book that made you throw up. Remember? I know you do!

Please, please always remember that I love you so much, and together we can get over anything. But, once again, you have nothing to prove to me, because you already are everything that a mother could wish for.

So, my darlings, no matter where you decide to live, in The United States, or in Mexico, the table in our home will be full of healthy, fresh, delicious food, and lots and lots of love.

Here's to our being healthy, loving and forgiving, wherever we may be, and never judging ourselves or others because of perceived differences,

su mami

The What And How Of Nutrition

Slow Death with a Knife and Fork

Food is life, and without it we die. We all know this simple truth. So, doesn't it stand to reason that the quality of our food will also impact the quality of our lives? We don't eat just to stay alive. We eat to have energy, to fuel our brains, to form our bones, and keep our teeth white and sharp, to give moisture to our skin, to feel healthy, and enjoy life. Yet, if we don't give our bodies the type and amount of food they need, when they need it, we are committing the equivalent of slow suicide with a knife and fork.

Does this statement sound like an exaggeration? It isn't. The purpose of eating is much more than to satisfy our hunger and stay alive. It is the nutrients in food, (or lack of them), that feed or starve our organs and blood cells. They either boost the immune system or deplete it, heal our bodies or attack them, lower blood pressure or cause hypertension, increase blood flow to the brain and heart or clog the arteries, and stabilize blood sugar levels or spike them.

It is food and only food that makes our hormones, which in return send messages to our cells so we can function. It is food that permits us to think, talk, move, laugh, breathe, reproduce, and cry. It is food that rebuilds, every hour of every day, the chemicals in our bodies as we deplete them.

Yet, not just anything we put into our mouths will do this vital rebuilding. Fake, packaged, or canned food won't. Sugar won't. Trans fats won't. Junk food won't. We need to eat real foods, the ones you can hunt, fish, grow, and harvest.

It's like being overdrawn on our bank account. We can't spend and spend and not make any deposits. If we spend more than we deposit, we eventually will go bankrupt. A deposit of fifty dollars on a one hundred dollar debt won't satisfy our debtors. The same goes for our bodies. If we spend a hundred symbolic dollars on stress or anger, a cup of coffee and a donut aren't going to do the job.

Will Somebody Make Up Their Mind ... Please?

How do we know which foods we can trust to rebuild and protect us against disease? Joan Rivers jokingly says that we never know who we can believe because we live in a nation that changes its opinion almost every day:

> "One day margarine is good for us, so we stop buying butter; then we're told to do the opposite because margarine has trans fats. We're told that chocolate causes acne and headaches, but then medical research discovers that it really has great benefits, such as helping with PMS, controlling blood sugar and boosting endorphins. However, it does have caffeine, which keeps us up and is addictive, yet a recent study said caffeine is actually a great antioxidant. The sun was in for a while because it's the best source of Vitamin D, which absorbs the calcium we lose as we get older, but now it's out because it causes cancer and wrinkles. Then someone said no and then yes and then possibly, then maybe not, maybe yes. We were all excited when olestra came out, the highly touted drug that substitutes fat, but now they say that it drains important nutrients from the body, may block natural digestion and causes diarrhea. At least everyone knows that salt is bad for you because it hurts the kidneys, but then another study came out saying that low salt levels are dangerous because we need the iodine. Researchers

never get it right the first time, and what are we supposed to do when even too much spinach can cause kidney stones, but not for everyone?"

From Ms. River's audio tape _"Don't Count the Candles"_.

Joan reflects a lot of the confusion and frustration we have surrounding nutrition. So, we need to know and listen to our own bodies, and understand the basic chemistry of how they work.

The Basics Of Nutrition

We can't turn on the TV, listen to the radio, or open a newspaper without reading something about the importance of eating healthy, losing weight, and consuming our five portions (or is it seven, now?) of veggies and fruit. But we continue to be the second fattest, (it seems that Australia just surpassed us), nation in the world and one of the unhealthiest in the modern world. Is it possible that many Americans don't know that a Big Mac is bad for you, even after the success of the movie, _"Supersize Me?"_

Could it be that there are people out there who want to lose weight, but just don't know how? Do they have a passionate "why", but just need the "what" and "how"? The answer is yes.

A Personal Story

When I was a volunteer with the Make-A-Wish Foundation, we bestowed a wish on a brother and sister who were twelve and thirteen, respectively, and who had Duchenne Muscular Dystrophy, a life-threatening illness that little by little steals away all lower mobility.

Their wish was to go to the beach. Pretty, amazing isn't it? They lived in San Diego, but had never seen the ocean. So, along with two other siblings and their mom and dad, we took them to the Del Mar beach, which is equipped with special wheelchairs that roll on the sand. The amazing and compassionate lifeguards gave them rides in their sand trucks, took them out in speed boats to see the dolphins up close, and gave them signed t-shirts and towels. The children shrieked with joy as they were pushed in the wheelchairs into the shallow part of the ocean and kept looking at their mother, as if to say, "can you believe this?" Yes, we completed our mission; it was a day they never would forget.

However, everyone in this family of five was extremely obese. The father had to carry the two children who suffered from this horrible disease wherever they went; onto and off of the truck, into and out of the speed boat, and so on. You could see the perspiration on his brow and hear the grunts of the extra human effort he had to make with every bend, every lift, and every release.

I would watch him and wondered how long he would be able to lift his children, victims of this rare disease. As the children grew and became weaker, his back or his heart, or both, would give out. He, too, was extremely obese, and I worried about what would happen to the whole family if he died prematurely from any of the life-threatening diseases that were weight or stress related.

So, with their permission, we sat down with them, using colored markers, and explained the risks of being overweight and of the dangers of their diet, which consisted mainly of fried food, soft drinks and refined grains. I also wrote three lists: one of food they could eat all they wanted, the second comprised food they could eat sometimes, and the third list was of food they should never eat. The family, who honestly never had heard this information, promised to follow our advice. They now had tools to take control of their weight and their lives. Finally, here was a solution to a life and death situation for them!

Here are the lists I gave them:

Eat More

Oat bran

Legumes (beans, lentils, nuts)

Fruit: what ever is in season and inexpensive (oranges, papaya, grapefruit, cantaloupe, watermelon, apples, berries)

Vegetables: especially the dark green and brightly colored ones (carrots, broccoli, kale, lettuce, string beans, bell peppers, beets, cauliflower, spinach, tomatoes)

Egg whites

Fish: seafood rich in omega-3 fatty acids yet low in sodium, saturated fat, and mercury ... herring, tuna, mussels, salmon, sardines (water-packed without salt), trout (farmed), and whitefish.

Eat Less

Ice cream (even non fat)

Red meat

Palm and coconut oil

Commercially prepared cookies, cakes, and pies

Man-made carbohydrates

Do Not Eat Or Drink

Soft drinks

Bacon

Sausage

Butter

Whole milk

Hydrogenated oil

Sugar

White Food (bread, rice)

Worrying About It When The Time Comes

My Make-a-Wish-Family didn't know, (but most of us do know), what is good and bad for us. We just don't want to change. Period. Like I said, I am no exception.

I know the sun is bad for me. But I love how it feels on my body and how it turns my pasty white skin into a golden brown tone. All of the sports I enjoy require me to be outdoors. Of course, I know the sun dries the skin and causes premature wrinkling and skin cancer, and I do use sunscreen.

But, since it takes years, sometimes decades, for those ugly brown age spots and wrinkles to surface, not to mention skin cancer I too have been guilty of pretending not to know what I know.

If cracks and age spots had surfaced after I had been out in the sun just one day, or a week, or even a month, I definitely would have been more cautious. If we smoked just one cigarette and then got lung cancer, I know no one would smoke. If we ate one meal high in fat and sugar, and then immediately got allergies or life-threatening diseases like diabetes or hypertension, everyone I know would give up on these foods, no matter how good they tasted.

> We not only want instant gratification; we demand instant results to make changes. And since it takes hundreds or thousands of cigarettes, McDonald hamburgers, and days in the sun to tear down our tissues, weaken our immune systems, and drive our endocrine systems crazy, we act as if we will be one of the exceptions and nothing will happen to us. To others, maybe. But not to us. We think we have the luxury of lying to ourselves and making excuses.

Below is a list of some excuses, which range from where we live to how we were brought up, to justify our unhealthy habits.

It's not my fault ...

It's geography: Only Californians who live in the sun jog because they want to show off their bodies.

It's economics: The wealthy are thinner and healthier because they can afford to eat organic food, go to private gyms, and pay for health insurance.

It's our parent's fault: This is the way my parents fed me, and what is good enough for them is good enough for me.

It's no fun: Vegetables and fruit, along with exercising, are just boring. Give me my comfortable chair, a beer, and a pizza, and I'm happy.

There's no time! We barely have enough time to fulfill all of our obligations, social engagements, and household projects, let alone shop and cook fresh food.

It's my reward. Food is the only thing I can give myself as a reward or compensation for a less than perfect life.

It's those mini portions. They would starve anyone.

It's in my genes: Either we have good ones or we don't. It's predestined. Everyone in my family is overweight.

"Get a life!" others exclaim, as they stuff another chocolate-covered marshmallow in their mouths, when I suggest fruit instead. "We only live once, let's enjoy it!"

With these self-limiting beliefs, I guess it isn't so hard to understand the lack of motivation to change.

Let's analyze and answer these excuses.

Geography: "Only Californians, and those in warm climates exercise and eat fruits and vegetables to show off their bodies."

Hundreds of Chinese men and women, who are known for their health and longevity, eat fresh food and meet in parks and do tai chi together.

Economics: "Only the rich can afford to go to gyms and eat organic and healthy food."

Water is cheaper than soft drinks, fresh vegetables cost less than a bag of nachos, walking is free ... and you, too, can go to a public park like the Chinese do.

No Fun: Brisk walking, roller blading, playing tennis, and having sex (which uses about 250 calories) is more fun than watching television (and you might even make some new friends).

'What's Good Enough for My Parents is Good Enough for Me': Well, is that what you really want? Do you really want to look like them when you are their age?

Healthy Food Tastes Bad: Sugar and high fat are sweet and smooth. But, is it worth it to get diabetes, heart disease, cancer, or dementia? There are grocery stores filled with healthy food. I am sure you can find something that whets your appetite. Have you tried peanut butter on a whole wheat bagel, or mashed avocado topped with a juicy tomato on wheat toast?

Tiny Portions: "Healthy food portions are too small and I'll starve."

It takes thirty minutes for our brains to register that we are full, so eat slower and chew longer. If you eat three, complete meals consisting of the three main food groups, and complement them with two healthy snacks, you won't go hungry. Also, drink lots of water, (half your body weight in ounces), in between meals.

OK, but **What About Time?** There are only 24 hours in a day, and it is physically impossible to do all that is needed to be healthy.

Lack of time is probably the best excuse of all, and I completely identify. But, if we don't make the time, the consequences will force us to. Make time, or you won't have any time left to make.

Different Strokes for Different Folks

There are certain nutrients that we all need, but because of different ages, stress levels, life styles, backgrounds, or geographic neighborhoods, it is possible to eat too little or too much of these same nutrients.

For example, Vannessa works with young children and lives in contaminated Mexico City. She needs more antioxidants, such as vitamin E, C, and B complex than most. Vivianne has asthma and allergies, so she has to substitute animal protein and dairy products with soy, fish, and nuts. Jennifer, has a very strong constitution and rarely gets sick, however she needs to take more ginkgo biloba and bicopa to help her memory, and regenerate the neurons she lost when she was sick.

My lungs are my weak point, so I need to take more Vitamin A and D, and because I am in post menopause, I also need to take bio-identical hormones, extra calcium, and selenium. I recommend you read "Vibrant Living", by Sally Karvich, and _"The Schwarzbein Principle"_, by Diane Schwarzbein, so you can understand your individual needs. Better yet, consult a nutritionist or holistic doctor whom you trust.

It's Later Than You Think!

Bottom line: It's just too much work! Denial and rationalization of what and who we might become when we reach our seventy-plus years might have made sense, even been psychologically necessary twenty years ago, because there was no purpose for dwelling on something we thought we couldn't do anything about. We didn't know then what we know now about the causes of mind/body degeneration, nor did we know that we can regenerate our minds and bodies, and reverse the aging process.

Even today, many of my contemporaries insist they are still relatively young and can't worry about something that might happen in the distant future; they'll worry about their body's decline if the time comes. Well, hold your breath, because for most of us tomorrow is here. At age forty-five we start to lose bone density, muscle mass, and billions of neurons.

Common Sense Nutrition

Eat a low-fat diet. Remember, what's good for the heart is good for the brain. Blood doesn't circulate well when it's full of fat.

Eat a diet with lots of nutrients. Fast food has been depleted of its nutrients, and only stresses your organs as they try to assimilate and eliminate artificial food.

Eat a relatively low-calorie diet. Eighteen hundred calories a day is sufficient. Calorie restriction is still the only proven method to enhance life span.

Eat a number of small meals and snacks throughout the day. (If you starve yourself trying to lose weight, your body will hold on to everything you eat, trying to protect you from perceived famine.)

Eat real food, not processed, canned, or pesticide-poisoned food. You will know if it's real if you can pick, gather, milk, fish, or hunt it. Most of it you will find in the grocery produce section.

Only make as many changes at one time as you can stick to. If you try to make too many changes, you will end up making none.

Never skip a meal. When you do, your adrenaline and cortisol levels increase, and you set yourself up for blood sugar chaos.

Build your meal around a protein. It can be lean meats, poultry, fish, eggs, or tofu.

Do not eat processed foods. If you are not sure what they are, consider processed foods to be anything that is canned or packaged or comes in a mix.

Eat smaller portions than you are used to eating.

Add carbohydrates that can be grown, picked, or harvested.

Choose seasonal fruits and vegetables with the most color.

Use healthy fats with omega-3 and omega-6 fatty acids instead of trans fats.

Drink lots of water in between meals instead of with them.

Read all labels. If you don't understand something, your body probably won't like it, either.

Always eat a nutritious breakfast, especially if you want to lose weight and keep it off.

Buy organic food as much as possible.

Consume at least three fish dishes a week.

Have Your Snacks And Eat Them, Too...

"But I get hungry during the day." That's actually a good sign, because it means your metabolism is working. However, that is no consolation when you just have to eat something, better known as a "snack attack", when you have to have something sweet or crunchy or you will just die. Here, size, once again, is the enemy.

Some Healthy Snack Ideas
(American Journal of Clinical Nutrition 2004;)

Peanut butter on a whole wheat cracker

Light cheese with a pear

Half an apple with 2 tsp of peanut butter

An orange and a few dry roasted nuts: 10 cashew nuts / 10 almonds

Half a small avocado

1 seven grain Belgian waffle

4 mini rice cakes with 2 tbs. low fat cottage cheese

1/4 cup fat-free ranch dressing with mixed raw veggies

1 small baked potato with 1/2 cup salsa and 2 tbs. fat free sour cream

1/2 cup frozen orange juice, eaten as sorbet

2 large graham cracker squares with 1 teaspoon peanut butter

3 handfuls of unbuttered popcorn, seasoned with herbs

4-6 ounces of no-fat or low-fat yogurt

Half a finger of string cheese with 4 whole wheat crackers

Statistics About Hydration
and the American Public

Seventy-five percent of Americans are chronically dehydrated.

Thirty-seven percent of Americans mistake the thirst mechanism for hunger.

Even mild dehydration will slow down one's metabolism.

One glass of water will shut down midnight hunger pangs.

Lack of water is the number one trigger of daytime fatigue.

Eight to ten glasses of water a day could significantly ease back and joint pain for up to eighty percent of sufferers.

Drinking five to eight glasses of water daily decreases the risk of colon cancer by forty-five percent, plus it can slash the risk of breast cancer by seventy-nine percent. A person who drinks five to eight glasses of water daily is fifty percent less likely to get bladder cancer. (Web MD.)

Supplements

Even if we are eating healthy, we don't know where or how the products we consume are grown. We need supplements because our soil is depleted of vitamins and minerals, and by the time food gets to our plates, it has been trucked, processed, dyed, freeze-dried, thawed, washed, cooked, colored, and depleted of its nutrients to make the food look good. So we are actually eating a cadaver.

Anyhow, it would take twenty oranges a day to get a single gram of Vitamin C, or twenty pounds of liver to get 50 mg of B6. We need supplements containing concentrated forms of nutrients such as vitamins, minerals, enzymes, amino acids, colostrum, and green juice products to overcome the harmful effects of pollution, radiation, and free radicals.

These tables detail the vitamins and minerals we need and why. (If this is too complicated, take a prenatal vitamin.)

Basic Vitamins

Vitamin D
600 IU. The sunshine vitamin helps bones use calcium and prevent fractures.

Vitamin B complex (B6, B12, folate)
Lowers homocysteine, which can contribute to Alzheimer's, heart attack, and stroke.

B12
100-1,000 mcg. Lack is associated with cognitive and memory decline.

B6
50-200 mg. Converts stored blood sugar into glucose, the brain's only fuel.

B1
50-100 mg. Is involved in innumerable metabolic processes in the brain.

Folic acid
400 mcg. Relieves depression, opens arteries in the neck and breaks down homocysteine, thought to be a precursor to Alzheimer's disease.

B3 Niacin
100-200mg. Manufactures neurotransmitters, calms us down, and lowers cholesterol.

B5
100-200 mg. Synthesizes the brain's primary memory neurotransmitter, choline.

Antioxidants To Fight Off Disease

Vitamin A
10,000-25,000 IU. Good for your skin and eyes. Note! Excessive Vitamin A can leach calcium.

Vitamin C
1 gram three times daily. Powerful anti-oxidant that protects us from oxidation, aging, and disease.

Vitamin E
300 mg. promotes longevity, improves immunity and promotes cardiovascular health

Minerals

Zinc
30-50 mg daily. Provides powerful anti-aging properties. You can't get enough from food.

Selenium
100 mcg. This is the most effective mineral antioxidant, boosts immunity and improves circulation.

Magnesium
400 mg. This is a powerful free-radical scavenger, promotes

circulation and decreases blood pressure. (Double or triple if you have heart disease, muscle pain, headaches, asthma, diabetes or kidney disease.)

Calcium
1,200-1,500 mg. Builds up bones and calms you down.

Preventative Tonics

Coenzyme Q-10
100 mg

Green Drink Chlorine
1,500-2,000 mg

L-carnitine
250 mg

Lutein
20 mg. Supports Visual Function

For Your Brain

Ginkgo biloba
30 mg three times daily

DMAE
50-100 mg

Lecithin
1,500 mg daily

Phosphatidyl serine
100-300 mg

Acetyl L carnitine
250 mg daily (take together with phosphatidyl serine)

Siberian ginseng
750-1,500 mg

Green tea
1 to 2 servings

Coenzyme Q-10
100 mg. Minimum formula for brain: lecithin + B5 + C.

The Basics: The Macro Nutrients

Protein

We need protein for growth, to build new tissue and muscle, replace old cells, signal enzymes to do work, form antibodies, and maintain healthy blood levels.

But.....

Too much of a good thing can be bad. During menopause and post-menopause, too much protein saps calcium from our bones. Divide your weight by three and you will get the grams that you ideally need.

Too much protein makes your kidneys and liver work too hard, depletes calcium from bones, and, if from animals, it is usually high in fat, and may cause dehydration.

What foods have protein?

Meat and poultry
Cheese
Fish and shellfish
Nuts and seeds
Soy products
Eggs

You can combine foods to get all of the amino acids in protein:

Beans and whole wheat tortillas
Pea soup and cheese
Soybean curd and rice
Baked beans and brown bread

To Do List for Proteins:

Eat only fresh meats. Avoid processed meats.
Use only nitrate-free and hormone-free meats.

Fats (Lipids)

Healthy Fats

Healthy fats surround and protect our organs, keep us warm, synthesize Vitamin D, maintain hormone balance and a healthy metabolism, keep us feeling full, slow down the absorption of proteins and carbohydrates, and help us to digest.

There are three types of healthy fats: saturated, monounsaturated and polyunsaturated. They are found in dairy products, cheese, meat, poultry, fish, and oils.

Recently, the fatty acids omega-3 and omega-6 have received lots of warranted good publicity. They represent the two major families of essential fats we need for basic functioning of our body, including blood clotting, blood pressure, immune function, blood sugar levels, fertility, reproduction, and replenishment of skin oils to speed healing, and decrease wrinkling. Omega-3 fats are found in fatty fish, (salmon, herring and mackerel), wild game, breast milk, ground flax seed, and omega-3 eggs.

Omega-6 fats are found in all of the oils, especially safflower, sunflower, and mayonnaise. They also can be found in large quantities in seeds, nuts, tofu, avocado, and poultry.

Since there are many more foods with Omega-6 fatty acids, you may have to supplement your diet with ground flaxseed to get adequate amounts of Omega-3. It is believed the ratio of omega-3 to omega-6 fatty acids is most important, using a 1:3 ratio. In other words, we need to eat at least 1 gram of Omega-3 for every 3 grams of Omega 6.

Foods With Healthy Fats

Avocado
Nuts
eggs
olives
flaxseeds
Seeds

Bad Fats

Not all fat is created equal. Fats are put into two categories: LDL and HDL

LDL: Think of L for lard or lousy ... meaning bad guy; takes up space and has unlimited storage; sticky fat forms plaque.

HDL: Think Happy and Ho ho ho ... meaning good guy. HDL fats roam around in the blood stream and get rid of LDL. They're heavy like a marble.

Do's And Don'ts Of Fats

Do: Use mostly monounsaturated fats for cooking, such as canola, sesame, grape seed, soybean, olive, and peanut oil.

Do: Keep fats refrigerated.

Do not: use polyunsaturated oils for cooking (corn, cottonseed, and sunflower oil).

Carbohydrates
(Sugar, Starches, and Fiber)

Provide energy
Conserve protein
Maintain healthy digestive systems
Reduce blood cholesterol levels (fiber)
Protect against gallstone formation
Provide a rich source of B vitamins
Contribute to skin, hair, eye and liver health
Help regulate appetite
Keep the brain and nervous system running optimally

What Foods Are Carbohydrates?

breads
legumes
sugary foods

alcohol
yogurt
grains
cereals
fruits
some vegetables: (artichokes, beets, butternut squash,
carrots, corn, green peas, okra, potato, pumpkin, yams.)

Fiber

Found in vegetables, fruits, whole grains, legumes
Prevents constipation
Decreases colon cancer
Decreases heart and artery disease

Sugar

Can cause excess weight and obesity
Can increase risk of heart disease (with fat)
Can cause diabetes.
Promotes tooth decay
Creates "the browning effect" which accelerates aging
and death

Why You Should Be Eating Good Carbohydrates

Carbs are a rich source of B vitamins and contribute to skin, hair,
eye, and liver health. They also help regulate appetite, and keep
the brain and nervous system running optimally.

Skimping on carbs can throw the body out of balance, because something it needs isn't showing up for work.

Too few carbs may lead to increased appetite, and insatiable cravings.

If eating a low-carb diet equals lots of saturated fat and cholesterol-heavy foods, these can increase your risk of high cholesterol, heart disease and cancer ... not to mention upping your risk of diverticulitis, an infection in the pouches within the colon, due to lack of dietary fiber.

Bigger Isn't Always Better

The French paradox refers to the fact that for some "inexplicable" reason, the French are able to consume buttery croissants, creamy brie, and decadent pastries and remain svelte. In fact, weight is not something the French are obsessed with or discuss much. Food is to be enjoyed among friends in a leisurely and unrushed manner. Yet, in the United States, where a third of our population is obese, it is a subject of constant worry and conversation. Could it be genetic? Or, perhaps food digests better when appreciated in a happy environment? The answer is right in front of our eyes on our plates. There is much more to eat, and studies have proven that if food is moderately palatable, people will eat it, be they French or American.

A study funded by The National Institute on Drug Abuse compared the size of restaurant meals, single-serving foods in supermarkets, and cookbook portions on both sides of the Atlantic. Their unbiased finding should not be a great surprise to those of us who have traveled abroad. The mean portion across all Paris establishments was twenty-five percent less than in Philadelphia, and the same was true for single-serving foods sold in supermarkets. For example, a candy bar sold in Philadelphia was forty-one percent larger than the same product in Paris, a soft drink was fifty-two percent larger, a hot dog was sixty-two percent larger and a carton of yogurt was eighty-two percent larger (see Breakthrough Digest, August 21, 2003).

So, yes, maybe we sin from a lack of will power, but we are only human. If you give it to us and it is good, we will eat it. To begin with, when you go to a restaurant, send away the bread ... and the butter. Then immediately ask for a doggy bag and put half or a third of the portion in it. If you are with someone, ask the waiter to divide one portion.

Yo-Yo Dieting

Up and down like a roller coaster your weight goes. One day you fit into a size eight, the next it's a size ten, but then for a while it's size six. This common practice is called yo-yo dieting and negatively affects your heart, your energy levels, and your future efforts at weight loss (according to the Women's Ischema Symptom Evaluation [WISE], funded by National Heart, Lung, and Blood Institute.)

> Weight cycling sets you up for binges. You're always either getting too many calories, which turn to fat, or your body is in deprivation mode from eating too little. Your metabolism is constantly thrown out of whack and never burns calories efficiently, which hampers any effort at weight loss (according to WebMD).

Fad Diets

They're not based on science, and their only reason is to lose weight, not long-term disease prevention or even day-to-day energy. You tend to feel too tired to exercise, irritable, and moody during a fad diet.

Depending on how wacky and lacking in nutrients the fad was, you may have lost lean muscle mass and bone density along with body fat. Building up muscle mass is easy by lifting weights, but getting back bone density is more problematic. Take calcium supplements, get moderate amounts of sun, and never go on a fad diet again!

Avoid Temptation

The focus of this book is on successful aging through intelligent choices, not on how to lose weight or be thin. I believe normal weight is a result of eating healthy and exercising. However, I would be remiss if I didn't acknowledge that being overweight is a concern of almost all of us, and it is the underlying cause of many degenerative diseases such as diabetes and hypertension. I also know that overeating is an epidemic in almost all societies, and as you can imagine I have given it a lot of thought to the underlying reasons.
There are many reasons why we overeat.

1. Hundreds of advertisements and images bombard us every day to consume unhealthy fast food and go to fast food restaurants.

2. We use food for emotional reasons: to numb loneliness, sadness, anger, boredom, etc.

3. Portions are larger than what we need for nourishment, but if they are in front of us, we will finish them.

4. We relate food to festive holidays and happy times

5. Eating is an excuse for getting together and celebrating.

6. Many ethnic groups equate eating large quantities of food as a demonstration of love and generosity.

It is not my purpose to delve into each one of these universal and understandable reasons for overeating and consistently gaining weight. But if these reasons keep us from our goal of leading healthy, energetic, confident, and joyful lives, then they need to be addressed.

I believe with all my heart that life is about lessons and choices. It's not about finding excuses, no matter how good the excuses are. It's about knowledge. It's about willpower. It's about taking responsibility and being accountable for 100% of our actions. It's about solutions.

Practical Solutions to Our Natural Tendency to Overeat

If it's in front of me, I'll eat it.

Tell the waiter to take away the butter ... and the bread.

Make a deal with yourself: You can eat small portions of what you love, just not at home.

Plan your meals ahead of time: Prepare them on the weekends and freeze them.

Have carrots and/or celery peeled and cut up in the veggie bin, but where you can see them. In most supermarkets you can buy bags of freshly cut apples, jicama, carrots, celery, or fruit plates. (Since I live alone, it is cost effective for me to go this route because I don't throw anything away, and it's as easy as opening the refrigerator door.)

Don't get too hungry. That means don't let more than five hours go by without eating, but don't eat before three hours. If you're hungry, you'll eat anything. So, if you know you are going to take a long road trip, or take an airplane, which means hours away from home, don't be tempted. Bring your healthy snacks with you. You will feel so much smarter than the other people who are spending far too much money to gain weight and get gas.

Bring a tote of almonds, trail mix, raisins, or unsalted nuts. Prepare them the night before you go anywhere.

Keep a glass or bottle of water with you at all times.

Every time you lose weight, take in your clothes, so if you gain weight they won't fit you.

Have snacks and eat them too.

As a rule of thumb, do not eat before three hours after a meal or more than five hours after a meal. Yes, easier said than done. Sometimes we just need a snack. As long as it is around 100 calories, you will be fine. Be aware of this fact, recently some food companies have come out with 100 calorie snacks. Please, as always look at the ingredients. I think you will find that although low in calories, they are high in unhealthy, artificial sweeteners and hydrogenated fats to give them shelf life.

Below is a list of healthy snacks that are not more than 100 calories. The secret is to balance them with a bit of protein, fiber, and healthy fat. The secret is to keep the portions small.

Some ideas for healthy low calorie snacks:

peanut butter on a whole wheat cracker
light cheese with a pear
half an apple with 2 teaspoons of peanut butter
an orange and a few dry-roasted nuts
10 cashew nuts
10 almonds
half a small avocado
1 seven grain Belgian waffle
4 mini rice cakes with 2 tablespoons low-fat cottage cheese
1/4 cup fat-free ranch dressing with mixed raw veggies
1 small baked potato with 1/2 cup salsa and 2 Tlbs. fat free sour cream
1/2 cup frozen orange juice, eaten as sorbet
2 large graham cracker squares with 1 teaspoon peanut butter
3 handfuls of unbuttered popcorn, seasoned with herbs
4-6 ounces of no-fat or low-fat yogurt
Half a finger of string cheese with 4 whole wheat crackers

Plan of Action

I really want you to make time to do the following action plan. You might feel that I am getting down to the basics, and you're right. Sometimes it just takes doing what we know we must do. So, please just don't read this. If it's late at night or you are starving, don't begin. It's best to begin your action plan when you're stomach is full, and you have at least a few, free hours.

Part I

1. Look in a magazine for someone your age and with your body type. Cut out a picture of her. Then look for a picture where you like how your face looks and cut it out. Paste your head on your new body.

2. Put her on your refrigerator with a magnet and then ...

3. Say to yourself or out loud, as you internalize the new you, "Every day in every way I am becoming healthier and stronger and closer to the woman I was born to be. It's only a matter of time and space."

Part 2

4. Get three or four large cardboard boxes.

5. Go through your kitchen cabinets and refrigerator and bid au revoir to the food that is keeping you from being HER ... you know, that beauty on your refrigerator. Now, I know it's like throwing away good and faithful friends. Many of these crunchy, creamy foods have comforted us when we were sad, celebrated with us when we were happy, and kept us company when alone. There were times when they took on a life of their own and were there for us when no one else was. Who could have imagined that at the same time they were robbing us of our health, energy, and years of life?

The rocky road ice cream that was there for you when John didn't call (but also put fat on your thighs); the potato chips that accompanied you when watching TV alone; (whose sodium content made you retain water); the butter that you put on your pancakes, just because you wanted to (and clogged your arteries) and yes, even the chocolate chip cookies that were always there awaiting you (because they had so many transfats that they lasted forever). It's time to say good-bye to them. Maybe not forever. You can go back to them later on if you like. But the closer you get to being that woman on the refrigerator, the less you will have anything to do with them.

6. Put everything in the cardboard boxes that is unhealthy, or that will age you prematurely. I have devised a technique that helps with closure, and makes saying good-bye bearable ... not easy, but bearable. Oh yes, I suggest you do this when alone. If not, others will doubt your sanity. Anyhow, give each object a kiss and thank it for whatever pleasure it has given you. Somehow this practice seems to help me when I am giving up something I wished I didn't have to. (It works great with pictures of old boyfriends too.)

As you read before, I know it is confusing to know what is healthy and unhealthy. So here is a partial list to help you in alphabetical order:

Put the following in a box ... or two ... or three, or more:

> artificial sweeteners (aspartame, saccharine, sucralose)
> barbecue sauces
> boxed cake mixes
> brown sugar,
> canned foods
> cookies,
> crackers
> croutons
> caffeinated beverages
> dried soups

flavored yoghurt
flour tortillas
gravies
fritos, nachos
imitation everything, like sour cream, mayonnaise, butter,
pudding
ketchup
margarine
oils (corn, coconut and palm)
pizza dough
pressured whip cream
processed meats, including pepperoni, salami and sausage
prepackaged vegetable juices in cans
potato chips
relishes,
soft drinks
toaster pastries
white bread and sugar

7. Throw them away, or give them away to someone who still lives in denial concerning the life and death importance of only putting live, healthy food into our bodies. If there is something on my list that you absolutely cannot live without, keep it and try to wean yourself off of it.

8. **Congratulate yourself. You have taken the first steps to being in control of your health, your future, and your destiny! Yea!** (Ok. By now you are probably not only tired, but thinking that you are going to literally die of hunger, since you threw away just about everything you eat.)

9. Go to the supermarket. It's time to begin your new regimen.

10. Buy food for one week.

At Your Favorite Super Market
Fill your basket with:

Organic, pesticide-free vegetables and fruit
Think DARK GREEN and BRIGHT COLORS. For example, beets, bell peppers, broccoli, brussels sprouts, cabbage, carrots, cauliflower, celery, chayote, chives, collared greens, cucumber, ginger root, green beans, hearts of palm, jicama, jalapeno peppers, kale, mushrooms, nopales, onions, parsley, radishes, squash, snow peas, shallots, spinach, tomatoes, turnips. Choose Fruit that is in season, and that you like, preferably apricots, berries, grapefruit, apples, jicama, papaya, avocado, cantaloupe, and oranges.

Add Some Grains
Brown rice, couscous, oatmeal, air kettle popped popcorn

From the Meat and Poultry Department
Buy fresh, hormone-free, antibiotic free, nitrate-free meats and wild fish, skinless chicken breasts, beef (if you must, but make it lean, and eat it no more than 2 times a week), wild salmon or albacore tuna, sardines, mackerel, or bluefish.

From The Refrigerator Section
Buy nonfat cottage cheese, cheese, (mozzarella, feta, ricotta, goat, muenster), tofu, free range eggs, natural yoghurt, (Horizon) natural juices, (Naked Juice); almond, rice or soy milk.

From The Grocery Aisles

Snack Food
A bag of almonds, walnuts, or salt-free nuts, string cheese, sugar free peanut butter. Trail mix, unsalted nuts, raisins, and, a treat that is no bigger than the circle you can make when your index finger and thumb touch. (That will be your reward, to be

eaten whenever you like during the day) These snacks are to be combined with fruit or vegetables, e.g. peanut butter on celery

Herbs and Spices
All that you like ... they are natural, and contain no sugar or toxins. My favorites are nutmeg, tumeric, cinnamon, and ginger.

Condiments
balsamic and other vinegars
garlic
low-sodium tamari soy sauce
olives
salsa

10. Buy a good, health-conscious cookbook. I recommend "The Schwarzbein Principle Cookbook."

11. Bring everything home and put it away. Now it's up to you how you will combine all of your treasures. I have a friend who treats himself like his most important guest.

Craig uses his best china and silverware, opens a fine red wine, and treats himself to a delicious green salad with avocado, spinach, boiled egg, walnuts, and feta cheese to go with his broiled salmon. Even if he is alone, he puts on his favorite music and never feels deprived. To tell you the truth, it's a great idea. But, I am too lazy. However, I am lucky because he often invites me.

Questions for you

▢ True ▢ False   My family members are all overweight
▢ True ▢ False   Some members are thin, and some are
                   overweight
▢ True ▢ False   My family uses food to celebrate

☐ True ☐ False   When I was little I was rewarded with food
☐ True ☐ False   I use food to comfort myself
☐ True ☐ False   I eat food when I am bored
☐ True ☐ False   I use food to make me feel better
☐ True ☐ False   I eat food when I am angry
☐ True ☐ False   I eat food because it tastes good
☐ True ☐ False   I continue to eat after I am full
☐ True ☐ False   I eat the most between 4:00 P.M.
                             and 10:00 P.M.
☐ True ☐ False   I consider myself to be overweight.
☐ True ☐ False   It is not my fault that I can't lose weight
☐ True ☐ False   I feel guilty when I break my diet
☐ True ☐ False   I am not happy with myself in general
☐ True ☐ False   I am not happy with my life in general
☐ True ☐ False   I blame my husband for my being overweight
☐ True ☐ False   I blame the television commercials for
                             lying to me
☐ True ☐ False   I blame my economic situation for
                             being overweight
☐ True ☐ False   Food is the only thing I have control over

Answer The Following Questions

I would like to lose weight because (I will have more energy)

Some diets I have tried are: (South Beach, Atkins, etc.)

The result I have had with these diets was: (I lost/didn't
lose weight)

I gained weight back because: (I went on a trip)

I kept the weight off because: (I looked too good to put it back on)

I need to lose _____lbs.

I want to lose_____lbs.

I will lose_____lbs.

I have lost_____lbs.

I am currently doing the following to lose/maintain weight:

I pamper myself by: (having a massage one a week)

I have given up on losing weight because; (nothing I do works)

I give to myself by: (having a Sees chocolate candy once a week)

I resent when people try to help me because: (I'm tired of it.)

In the past when I have lost weight, I have: (had more energy)

If I could lose weight I could: (go to Europe)

If I could lose weight I could:

Come on. Think big! If I could lose weight I could:

If I would lose weight I would:

If I would lose weight I would:

If I would lose weight I would:

The family rule about weight was/is: (it's more important to enjoy food than to be thin)

The first time that I knew I was overweight was when:
(I compared myself to my sister)

My favorite foods are:

My biggest meal is:

My favorite meal is:

I am willing to sacrifice the following foods:

I am not willing to sacrifice the following foods:

I think the most about my body image when:

I compare myself with_____ because:

I would like to look like_____because:

I don't go to _____or_____ because:

I share my feelings about my weight with _____

When I look in the mirror I see:

Weight Watchers is so effective because you realize your thoughts, needs, and fears concerning food are more common than you ever imagined.

You can answer these questions by yourself, but I suggest that you get a group of friends together and share your answers. You will realize you are not alone, and at the same time create a support system.

Something To Think About

Many of us are so hung up on eating, dieting, cheating, and eventually giving up, that we've forgotten the art of enjoying good food. Once again, we can learn from the French who enjoy food and don't worry about calories.

1. Recall mealtime in your childhood home. How have those early experiences affected the way you eat today?

2. Imagine you're having your last meal on earth, and

your nearest and dearest are there to share it with you. Describe the menu, the table setting and the people around the table. Is there anything preventing you from inviting them over for dinner next week?

3. Even the most disciplined eater lapses at times. When you sneak-eat, what foods do you choose? List them. What would it take to let yourself enjoy a treat guilt-free now and then?

4. In many spiritual traditions, food preparation is a form of meditation or prayer. Visualize your kitchen before meals. Is the atmosphere calm and respectful, or chaotic and rushed? How could you make food preparation a sacred act, or at least more peaceful and uplifting?

5. Remember, how you nourish your body reflects what you think about yourself, and how you feed your soul. If you believed you were feeding your soul, not just your body, how would it change the way you eat?

All of these results, and more, are a result of what you choose to put on your knife and fork. Your birthday will come next year, but biologically speaking, you won't have to show it.

In conclusion, this is the only body that you have. By putting healthy nutrients into it, you will find that your entire life will change. You'll have more vitality, self esteem, sleep better, and feel lighter. You will also see an improvement in your thinking, muscle tone and skin texture, and experience a greater resistance to colds and flu.

Websites For Health

www.healthfinder.gov (links to 1,800 health-related organizations)

www.medlineplus.gov (access to National Library of Medicine)

www.mediconsult.com (information on chronic conditions and autoimmune diseases)

www.healthywomen.org (information on women's health issues)

www.drinkbetterwater.com (a list of good water sources)

www.familydoctor.org (American Academy of Family Physicians)

www.acefitness.com (American Council on Exercise)

www.nal.usda.gov/fnic/foodcomp (nutritional data on more than 1,000 foods and their caloric, carbohydrate, vitamin, mineral content)

www.consumerlab.com (subscription-based to identify the best quality health and nutritional products through independent testing)

www.nnfa.org (National Nutritional Foods Association directs you to the nearest health retailers in your city)

www.springerlink.com (information for researchers in biomedicine, life science and more)

www.complementarynutrition.org (2,500 practitioners with an interest in the role of alternative therapies and dietary supplements)

"All the strength you need is within you.
Don't wait for a light to appear at the end of a tunnel.
Stride down and light the bloody thing itself."

~ Sarah Henderson (Australian Cattle Woman)

Chapter Six

Menopause
(July 2005)

Dear Vivianne,

When you were six months in utero, I entered an unmarked intersection driving a Volkswagen beetle, and was hit by four cars, then slammed into a post. The impact jolted me into the passenger's seat, where I sat covered in blood ... afraid and confused. A young man passing by directed others to call the Cruz Roja, and took it upon himself to stay with me and be my guardian. He held my hand as the ambulance rushed me to the "Ingles", and it was his conversation that kept me from losing consciousness as we wove through the congested streets of Mexico City. I remember repeating like a broken record, "Mi bebe? Mi bebe? Como está mi bebe?"

When I arrived at the hospital, Antonio and the whole family were already there, all with worried and anxious looks on their faces. The doctor had told them you didn't have a heartbeat. Your Auntie Maris and Yvonne, along with your dad, stayed with me all night, anxiously and patiently waiting for me to abort you.

Obviously, the doctors were mistaken! We left the next day ... both of us!

When we reached the ninth month, it appeared you didn't want to come out into such a violent world. I remember your Auntie Maris calling me twice a day, worried that the contractions hadn't begun. When we got to the tenth month, the doctor decided it was time to insist you make your appearance.

Since then, we have called you our "miracle child," not only because we were told you wouldn't live, but also because of all the miracles that you perform for others. I believe with every fiber of my being there would have been less joy and laughter and more sadness if Vivianne Nacif had not blessed this earth with her endless hours of love and volunteer work.

Each time I think of your miraculous birth, Vivi, I am reminded of how unwise I would have been to believe what the doctors said. Deep down, I knew that you would be born perfect.

How is it possible that my miracle baby is now getting married and will one day soon, si Dios quiere, have her own baby? For as often as I tried to stop time with our "remember, remember, remember," it has passed so quickly.

I feel that today on your wedding day, I should say something unforgettable, memorable, deep, profound. After all, that's what mother's do. But what can I say to you, what advice can I give you? We have talked in depth about the meanings and symbolism of the four sacred transitions of a woman's life: menstruation, marriage, pregnancy, and motherhood.

Each sacred passage has an importance of its own in a woman's life, as it prepares the way for the next one. We celebrated your first menstruation with flowers and hugs. I remember your questioning face when I brought you the bouquet, for at the moment you didn't understand the privilege of the red stain on your clothes. Today, I rejoice as I envision you, so tall and graceful, in your wedding dress, as you walk down the pier in Puerto Morelos. From the moment I saw that wooden plank pier from my bedroom widow, many months ago, I knew that would be the place you would take your marriage vows.

And one day, si Dios quiere, you will wear a beautiful stomach, cushioning my future grand child. I hope I will be by your side to watch your child grow in your body and relive many " remember, remember" times together. But, chances are I won't be here to celebrate with you the last, major, female rite of passage, menopause. So, although not the traditional one, I get to do the mother-daughter pre-wedding message after all. Believe it or not, I am going to talk about what is euphemistically known as "The Change."

Vivi, you and I have talked about how much you look forward to getting pregnant. As you step toward this new beginning in your life, I find that I, too, am stepping into a new phase of life, although my beginning is marked, not by marriage and childbirth, but by post-menopause, and a newfound freedom.

Menopause as you know is when our bodies, little by little, stop producing estrogen, and our reproductive years end.

Sadly, it is treated by many women of my generation with dread and secrecy, because historically we were taught that women were put on earth to reproduce, and when we no longer could, we were worthless. I would hope that today, all women realize we are so much more than our wombs, and our ability to conceive.

However, just as pregnancy can be a hormonal roller coaster, so is menopause, often causing the infamous night sweats, insomnia, and hot flashes. Not much fun! At first I listened to the doctors when they prescribed the synthetic hormones, Premarin and Pempro to relieve these common menopausal symptoms. I knew I needed to compensate for the diminishing levels of the sex hormones: estrogen, progesterone and testosterone.

However, my intuition told me that something wasn't right, and as always, was soon confirmed. In my studies in female biology at the university, I discovered that synthetic hormones are actually derived from the urine of a pregnant mare. The receptors in women's bodies don't recognize these foreign elements, so they don't bind.

As the doctors were wrong about your birth, they were wrong about synthetic hormones, too. If I had followed their advice and taken synthetic hormones, I would have heightened my risk for cancer, heart attacks, blood clots, gallbladder disease, and so many other things! What could I do? We need our hormones! Estrogen itself has over three hundred benefits, and progesterone and testosterone all add up to a woman who is energetic, sexual, and strong. I wanted to keep being that kind of woman.

Just as I felt intuitively that you would be born, Vivi, I knew there must be a better way to live the second half of my life. I researched and asked everyone I knew, and eventually I discovered bio-identical hormones. These are hormones derived from the wild yam or soy plant. They are exact matches to our bodies' receptors! I was so elated but confused to discover that most doctors don't prescribe bio-identical hormones simply because large drug companies don't market them. They are not patented, so these companies can't control the market and make a lot of money.

You cannot imagine how angry I was to realize that my health, (not to mention the health of most women), is being compromised simply because there is a low profit margin associated with bio-identical hormones.

One reason that I'm telling you this, Vivi, is to show you how important it is for women to take responsibility for their own well-being. No matter what, please always question. When someone tells you it can't be done, or it isn't going to work, ask, "Why?" Find out the truth. You are living evidence that the truth is completely different from the "official story."

As for me, I am sixty-one. I have learned menopause is a sacred chapter in my life, and is in any woman's life. It is the beginning of a new way of being. Women are spiritual, sexual, and intellectual. We are far more than the sum of our ovaries! We can have a limitless life where the quality of our moments, days, and years continue to enhance instead of decline with the passage of time. I dug down deep and found a way to continue living my life as a balanced, healthy, strong woman. I found compounding pharmacists who specialize in providing safe bio-identical hormones. Once I experienced their benefit, it was as if I were giving birth to myself.

My darling, I gave birth to you, I watched you grow, and now I see you move into your own sphere with Juan by your side. And soon you will have children of your own. And this, my sensitive and loving miracle child, is what I wish for you when that miracle occurs.

I wish for you a generous child, who gives you the gift of love, and makes you feel proud every day of your life. I wish for you a loving child, who not only makes you feel that you are a good mother, but one worthy of admiration.

I wish for you a giving child, who uses her unique talents to help others and make this a better world. I wish for you a supportive child, who is the first to attend any of your activities, and will always give you a standing ovation. I wish for you a playful child, who will fill your life with surprises that make you cry for joy. In other words, I wish for you what you have given to me, a child just like you.

And finally, on this, your wedding day, let me finish this unconventional letter, with a traditional wish: May you experience eternal joy and love, and also patience, strength, and wisdom for the difficult times that will inevitably come. And my beautiful Vivi, I don't have to wish that you find a man that will be by your side to support you during these times, because tomorrow, you will unite your life with such a man forever.

My dearest, follow your heart, follow your intuition, ignore the nay-sayers, and you will continue to lead a miraculous life.

I love you more than words could ever hope to say,

tu mami

P.S. "Follow your intuition, ignore the nay-sayers" were the last words of this letter. Today, one year and one month later, you did just that. The nay-sayer in this case was the result of a home pregnancy test. But, you didn't believe it when the result was negative. Your intuition told you that your child was already growing in you. You knew you were pregnant, no matter what the result of the test indicated. So, yesterday you took it again, and your intuition was confirmed. You and Juan are going to have a baby!

Vivianne, you have been more than a daughter. You have been my friend, my adviser, my helper, my strength. And now my darling, you are about to embark on the most exciting and wonderful journey of your life. You have never known love like the one you are about to feel. And as you go through pregnancy, the second sacred passage of a woman's life, I will be beside you, knowing that my miracle child is about to experience her own miracle. Such is the privilege of a mother's ... and soon to be ... grandmother's life!

The What And How Of Menopause

Menopause: (Meno: Latin, Meaning Month, Pause: End)

Menopause really is the core issue behind a woman's aging process. Physiologically, it is when the brain sends a message to the pituitary and tells it to, little by little, stop making the hormone estrogen in the ovaries. The ovaries in turn dry up, menstruation ends, thus terminating the reproductive years of a woman.

Psychologically, many women experience menopause as the symbolic end of their lives. Yet, the reality is quite the opposite. Menopause is only the end of our ability to have children. It can be the beginning of a new and wonderful time in our lives; new opportunities, life styles, careers, and if we like, newly defined romantic relationships.

> Menopause is a process, and can take many years; usually beginning in our forties and ending in our mid-fifties. These years are known as peri-menopause. During this time, although we continue to menstruate irregularly, hormones are playing havoc with our minds and bodies. It is during peri-menopause that many women experience insomnia, weight gain, hot flashes, night sweats, fatigue, and confusion.

Post-menopause is when our hormones finally settle down, and we enter a new stage that Margaret Mead calls postmenopausal zest (PMZ). Post menopause occurs after one complete year without a period. Many women believe it is no longer necessary to continue taking hormonal replacement therapy (HRT) at this time, but our bodies never cease to contain and need our hormones to function adequately, and in balance.

Our bodies have a complicated communication system, with hormones acting as messengers between the different cells and systems of the body. Our hormones regulate all the biochemical processes in our body. If your hormones are not delivering the right messages, in the beginning you might barely notice it, but as time progresses, this imbalance will cause accelerated metabolic aging and will end in a degenerative disease of aging, such as arthritis, osteoporosis, even cancer.

For you to remain healthy, you need to keep your hormones balanced so they can communicate effectively with each other and with your cells. But life itself is anti-balance, and our hormones are constantly changing to meet our daily requirements.

> Since all of life is about the balance between tearing down and building up, producing new hormones requires us to eat food that has the material our bodies need to make hormones. Since hormones are made primarily from proteins, cholesterol, and essential fats, eating a balanced diet is essential for keeping up the production of hormones.

Every time we inhale nicotine, spend hours in the direct sun, eat "dead" or toxic food (most of which is found on our grocery shelves, because they are processed to a point where they have very little nutritional value) or refined sugar, we are tearing down. The question is, "What are we doing to build up?" If we are proactive in our diet, stress management, exercise, and balancing our hormones, then we are building up and combating the aging process at the same time.

The Four Stages of The Third Act

In the same way that menopause does not equal old, it's important not to cluster every mature person into the same category. A fifty-five-year-old grandmother is very different from her seventy-five-year-old counterpart. For clarity on the aging process, let's take a closer look at what can be referred to as the third act. (Of course, the first being youth and the second, middle age.) The third act, according to "50+ Marketing", by Jean-Paul Treguer, has four, mini stages.

1. **The Masters (50-59 years):** The youngest baby boomers are still sexy and in good health, thanks to options such as hormone replacement therapy, cosmetics, plastic surgery, more money, (often from an inheritance), and the possibility of recommitting and renewing lost opportunities and dreams.

2. **The Liberated (60-74 years):** Relieved of the roller coaster symptoms of hormones during menopause, we have internal peace at post-menopause, and lots of time to do whatever we want. We are more tolerant, serene, compassionate, and non-judgmental. At the same time, we can be a bridge between the generations, bringing them together.

3. **The Peaceful (75-84 years):** With some exceptions, this is the beginning of old age. This is when most of our bodies break down with the degenerative diseases of aging, especially if we have been mistreating them.

4. **The Elderly (85+ years):** Although most of us are widowed, it can be a time of gratitude and acceptance. The diseases of the aging, especially Alzheimer's,

represent the biggest challenge. If we have taken good care of our bodies and minds, and have been generous and loving, we likely will be surrounded by our loved ones, in our own homes, when we take our last breath.

"I know I am in a whole other stage when I prefer a good result from a bone density test than a night of great sex with Denzel Washington; when I realize that the drapes or new set of dishes I buy will likely be the last ones that I'll ever buy; when I can't call myself middle-aged because that's what my children are, and when the people I used to discuss Marcel Proust with are discussing inheritance taxes and living wills."
(Judith Viorst, Forever Fifty)

A Personal Story

I hate being a victim! So often ... too often ... we are unsuspecting victims of "what everybody knows," (concepts, stories, opinions, beliefs, things?) which we have heard so often and from so many "experts", that we accept as fact or truth. Since I accepted the information in traditional books and what everyone knew, I took synthetic hormones (Premarin). After ten years I stopped, because everyone said the danger for breast cancer skyrocketed every additional year after the first ten. I didn't question what everyone knew. This was common knowledge, that people like me, who were educated and well-read, knew.

My boyfriend at the time didn't agree with my decision, and begged me to get back on my hormones. I screamed at him (I was doing a lot of that lately) for being so selfish and not caring if I got cancer, as long as I was in a good mood. (In hindsight, his plea wasn't such an absurd request.)

But, in the middle of my accusations, there was this little voice
I often hear when I need to calm down. This time it suggested,
"Maybe you don't have to choose; maybe you can take your
estrogen and be healthy, too."

Of course, I never let him know I was going to study my options. But
this time, I didn't want to be right. I wanted to be happy (and sexy).
The rest is history ... as is the boyfriend ... although I have to thank
him for being instrumental in making me happy instead of right, by
challenging me to proactively discover bio-identical hormones.

My first knowledge of bio-identical hormones was when I was on
the Internet at one of my favorite sites, Power-surge.com. There,
about five years ago, I discovered that bio-identical hormones are
synthesized from the wild yam, and once combined in a laboratory
to fit our specific needs, they behave exactly as our own hormones,
without the toxic side effects of synthetic hormones.

Soon after learning about these yam-synthesized hormones, I
gave a speech on menopause, and was approached by a generous
and knowledgeable nutritionist who offered to give me my saliva
test for free. The results showed what could be expected for a
woman of my age: low levels of all the sex hormones.

Once I started to rub what I call the magic elixir on my inner
thighs, the change was astonishing. It was as radical as going
from feeling dead to being alive again. The touch of a man's
hand on my body once again activated those wonderful
sensations that had been dormant, but now ... again ...
culminated in ecstasy. I started sleeping. I was at peace ...
not nervous or agitated. In fact, I believe it is thanks to my
bio-identical crème that I can be here in Puerto Morelos,
Mexico, all by myself, without a television or really anything
but my books, music, and writing, for months on end, feeling

completely content. (Well, except for my fantasizing about finding a man who will enjoy my newly discovered libido!) I am so grateful I didn't accept "what everyone knows and does", and found the truth for myself!

The Truth Is

The truth is, my hormones can and should be balanced so I don't have to go through menopausal symptoms such as night sweats, mood swings, vaginal dryness, and lowered libido.

The truth is, I am much more likely to die from a heart attack than from breast cancer, since no one in my immediate family had breast cancer.

The truth is, there is no logical reason to "tough menopause out"!

The truth is, if my hormones are balanced, and I eat healthy and exercise, I will most likely live to be over ninety, and enjoy my life with passion and joy.

The truth is, if you are lucky enough to begin living a healthy life and are in your thirties, your life span will be at least twenty years longer than mine.

The truth is, I wish I had known when I was thirty what I know today.

The truth is, I had heard only one side of the story.

Hormones Revisited

Let's go back to what is going on in our bodies during menopause. Our brain sends a message to our pituitary, which in turn tells our ovaries to little by little stop making the sex hormones, estrogen, testosterone, and progesterone, since we are getting too old to get pregnant. This was a pretty good plan I guess at the time, because women didn't live much past reproduction years.

Today, however, considering we reach menopause at about fifty, we will have at least thirty more years of life. So, don't you agree it's not such a good idea after all, to live without the benefits of these life-giving sex hormones?

The Sex Hormones

Estrogen

Estrogen offers over three hundred benefits to our bodies. Among them, it increases HDL (good cholesterol which greatly diminishes the possibility of heart attacks), lowers LDL (bad cholesterol), speeds up our metabolism, skims plaque from our arteries, keeps our bones strong, makes our bodies flexible, strengthens our neurotransmitters, helps us to sleep, and heightens our moods and attitude. There are twenty-four different estrogens, but we are mainly concerned with three:

Estradiol (E2): Made in our ovaries before menopause, it is the most powerful of the three, and its loss causes night sweats, insomnia, hot flashes, and bloating. However, an excess of E2 can cause cell division and breast cancer.

Estrone (E1): We continue to make this estrogen in our fat cells during post-menopause. That's why it is important not to become too thin during this time of life.

Estriol (E3): This estrogen only exists when we are pregnant, and is found in the placenta. Estriol is thought to be a deterrent for breast cancer, and represents no danger to our bodies. It also helps to keep our vaginas moist.

Progesterone

This hormone is produced when the egg leaves the ovary and leaves a follicle called nervioso corpus luteum, which is converted into progesterone. It counteracts the thickening of the lining of the uterus caused by estrogen, (the possible cause of uterine cancer), because if pregnancy doesn't occur, the progesterone level automatically goes down, and the whole lining is shed. We get our periods.

Progesterone improves our sleep, calms us down, eliminates water retention and weight gain, stimulates new bone growth, protects against cancer, and normalizes the libido.

Testosterone

Previously thought of as just a hormone that men needed, today we know that testosterone is also a female sex hormone. We need it not only for its positive effects on our libido, but also for increased energy level, and to create new bone mass.

Testosterone is carried in the blood, most of it attached to a protein known as sex hormone binding globulin (SHBG). Only a tiny amount of testosterone is unattached to protein or free in the plasma. Ninety-seven to ninety-nine percent of women's testosterone is attached to protein at any given time.

Both testosterone and estrogen are carried on the same protein. Estrogen actually stimulates the production of more SHBG, which then binds up still more of the testosterone, leaving less testosterone to be free to work on cells. This explains why taking supplementary estrogen at menopause can tie up a little more of whatever testosterone we may still have, sometimes tipping the balance and causing symptoms of testosterone deficiency.

Only if taken in excessive amounts can testosterone cause excessive muscle growth or facial and body hair.

Tri-Estrogen and Progesterone

This compound is the perfect combination of the three estrogens plus progesterone. What makes it so beneficial is the proportion: one part estradiol, one part estrone, and eight parts progesterone, the same combination you had when you were thirty-five.

Possible Side Effects of Synthetic Hormones

Prempro
For every 10,000 women taking Prempro each year,

Eight more will develop breast cancer.
Seven more will have a heart attack or other coronary event.
Eight more will have a stroke.
Eight more will have blood clots in the lungs.

Premarin

Risk of breast cancer
Risk of uterine cancer
Water retention
High blood pressure
Allergies
Diminished libido

Provera

Depression
Acne
Change in weight
Nausea
Allergic reaction
Headache

Another Personal Story

When I returned to the United States from Mexico, I wanted to make up for all of the years that I wasn't allowed to interact with the world. But, what I most yearned to do was be able to move my body, work out and exercise. I equated physical movement with freedom.

So, I rode my bike up steep hills; I went to the gym every day, worked out intensely for an hour and a half; and I race-walked along the cove in La Jolla. I thought that I was in great condition, and I probably would have been OK if I had regenerated by eating right and/or sleeping. But, I was doing neither. I didn't know it, but I was in the throws of peri-menopause and didn't sleep for days. I wanted to have low body fat, so I barely ate. And yes, I was thin; a thin bomb waiting to get a degenerative disease because I was tearing down, not building up!

After about seven years, instead of feeling strong and euphoric and enjoying my newly found body and freedom, little by little, I started to notice subtle changes. My hands shook all the time. I could barely lift a mascara wand, much less free weights. I evacuated every two to three hours, resulting in my eventually weighing under ninety pounds. People would tell me that I had a scared look on my face. Then, I started to see everything double, and my eyes would suddenly feel as if grainy acid had been thrown into them, so I could no longer drive, let alone get on stage as a motivational speaker. I was close to death and I didn't even know it! Thanks to the psychiatrist I started to see, (because of my insomnia), I was diagnosed with an autoimmune disease called Graves disease, which causes the thyroid to secrete too many hormones, and for some inexplicable reason also deforms the eyes. This time, as every person with a life threatening disease knows, is very frightening. When you're in the midst of illness, you don't see the gift.

The gift was the lessons I learned about myself, and that I am sharing with you. As Rachel Naomi Remen says in, "Kitchen Table Wisdom", "Perhaps every 'victim' is really a survivor who does not know it yet."

It is obvious to me that by overextending my body's resources, and not rebuilding, I caused myself to get sick. In fact, I strongly believe that autoimmune diseases such as MS, lupus, Graves, and others, are often directly related to life-style choices.

Today, at age sixty-one, I have completely recovered from Graves Disease. I had orbital surgery on my eyes, and thanks to an expert team of doctors, I no longer have diplopia (double vision) nor do I look scared, nor do I feel like there is sand in my eyes. I have retained my thyroid, and no longer take any medicine. My primary treatment centered on changing my way of acting, living, and thinking. I know that I no longer have the luxury of being stressed, or of over extending myself without rest, or of blaming myself for past or present things I can't change. Gratefulness, compassion, love, and peace are my companions.

The What and How of Bio-Identical Hormones

According to Dr. Diana Schwarzbein in her book, "The Schwarzbein Principle II", prescribing a bio-identical hormone, after taking blood or saliva tests, is not an open-and-shut matter. Many other things must be taken into consideration: personal history, individual desires and complaints, and so on. At the same time, there is no magic number that tells us exactly how much of each hormone we need. Sometimes it is trial and error. All of this takes time, time that most doctors don't have, not because they are selfish or mean, but because of insurance demands and patient overload. For most doctors, time is a luxury they don't seem to have. So search for a doctor who understands how important it is to tweak your hormones in order to find what works best for you.

Once that is done, you will not believe how wonderful, how young, how vital, and how sexual you will feel. Yet, if you do not want to feel sexual, your designer program can diminish the amount of testosterone or progesterone. I guess you can think of it like this: You can go into a department store and choose a dress that isn't your size and wear it. It won't fit you, but it will cover you, if that is all you want. Or, you can go to a designer and have her take your measurements and make a dress that will fit you perfectly, so you will look the best that you can.

The doctor not only gives you a blood test, she also talks with you at length and finds out how you feel, and what has changed in your life. She talks to you again in three months and in six months.

Steps to Follow

Step 1: Make an appointment with your gynecologist for a fifteen to thirty-minute hormone consultation. Make sure it is in her office with your normal clothes on, not in a backless gown, so you can feel as an equal with her or him.

Step 2: Be proactive and have all pertinent information written down: your symptoms, concerns, your past history, and family history, what you have tried, what has worked and what hasn't, and how you would like to feel.

Step 3: Since most of us still have a hard time being assertive, be assured that you have the right to make your own decisions about your own body. If you feel that your health provider isn't listening, or if she tells you there are no alternatives, or that you have to grin and bear your symptoms because they will eventually pass, thank her for her opinions and end the appointment. It is time to look for a doctor who is more open and informed.

Step 4: Once you have found a doctor, (more on where and how to find an appropriate doctor at the end of this chapter), she will do a blood panel to test your hormone levels. (I strongly suggest that all young women have a hormonal panel done before they enter peri-menopause so they can have a basis for comparison in the future.)

If you cannot locate a doctor in your area, there are other options.

1. If you have a computer, go to these web sites:

www.power-surge.com This is an informative and comprehensive site on menopause. Click on "Bio-identical hormones." There you will find the compounding pharmacy they recommend.

www.womentowomen.com You can have a phone consultation with their health professionals, or become a patient in their clinic. Call 1-800-340-5382 or 1-800-798-7902.

Their laboratory of choice is Great Smokies Diagnostic Laboratory (www.gsdl.com). They, too, will give you a list of healthcare   providers near you. Their phone number is 1-828-252-9303

www.womensinternational.com This site lists well established compounding specialists, or call 1-800-279-5708. They also can provide an information packet for you and your doctor.

www.naturalwoman.org This is Christine Conrad's (menopause specialist) web site for more referrals.

2. If you are near, or can to travel to La Jolla, California, I recommend you visit my doctor, Dr. Joe Filbeck, at his medical spa. For appointments please dial 1-858 457-5700, or go to his web site: www.palmlajolla.com

3. Another wonderful option is the Berman Center in Los Angeles, and soon in Chicago, where the renowned television celebrity and sexologist, Laura Berman, focuses on women's sexual health and menopause management using bio-identical hormones. For an appointment, you can call 1-800-709-4709 or go to her web site: www.bermancenter.com

Questions

How can I buy bio-identical hormones?

Here is a site that lists compounding specialists;

www.naturalwoman.org, or call: 1-800-279-5708

The site also can provide an information packet for you and your doctor. Find a doctor who understands and knows about bio-identical hormones. She will do either a saliva or blood test to determine your unique hormonal needs. She then will write a prescription to a compounding pharmacy, which will combine only the hormones that you need in the exact doses that you need. Bio-identical hormone replacement therapy (BHRT) has been around for over twenty years. However, most mainstream, health practitioners are either not aware of it, or have been trained to prescribe synthetic hormones like Premarin and Prempro (pregnant mare's urine). These doctors want the best for you, but probably didn't get much training in sex hormones in medical school. (It's hard to believe that women's health issues have only begun to be addressed in the last five years.) The drug companies probably have convinced your doctor that their synthetic hormones are the most trustworthy because they have been around for so long, and there is no reliable alternative. This reasoning is not true.

Cost: $60 to $80 every two months.

Blood test: $250.

How often should I re-test?

How often to re-test is different for every woman. It will depend on your medical history, and how you are feeling. Some women need to change their dosage every six months; others can go years using the same dosage. Once again, women in their thirties, like my daughters, should have their hormonal tests taken now, so they will have a base line to work with, saving them lots of time and unnecessary suffering later.

So, it's up to you. It makes so much sense to me to support our bodies naturally as well as feel the best that we can using the lowest doses. In other words, using bio-identical hormones. I know it is so much easier just to get a general prescription filled by your gynecologist, and I applaud you for going the extra mile. Don't give up. You won't be sorry.

I've been taking synthetic hormones for a long time. Is it too late for me?

Never!

More Web Sites and Pharmacies

The Great Smokies Diagnostic Lab performs tests for doctors to determine the levels of bio-identical hormones a woman needs. If you contact them and ask for a list of doctors who use their services in your area, they will send you a list via e-mail with names, phone numbers, and cities. Here is the web site:

www.gsdl.com (home page)

https://www.gsdl.com/secure/contact/ (contact form)

Dr. Patricia Allen has formed an organization called Women's Voices for Change, (WVFC), to promote the concept that menopause is not an ordeal to be weathered, but a singular opportunity in a woman's lifetime. The purpose sounds a lot like this book ... to foster the image of the New Menopausal woman as one of wisdom, creativity, sensuality, and determination.

Books that view all cycles of a woman's life as a sacred passage:

Starck, Marci.
"Women's Medicine Ways."

Harrigan, Bonnie.
"Red Moon Passage: The Power and Wisdom of Menopause."

Lee, John R.
"What Your Doctor May Not Tell You About Menopause."

Meisenbach, Kristi.
"The Seven Sacred Rites of Menopause."

"As our bodies meet,
I don't want you to feel
I'm the most important thing in the world,
I want you to feel the world
— which I stand for —
is your friend."

~ Ellen Reiss

Chapter Seven

Sex

(July 2005)

Dearest Vivianne,

I know you expected this letter from me. You knew I would document your unforgettable, unique, and beautiful Mayan wedding. What we didn't imagine is that I would be writing to you from Jenny's house in Mexico City.

It's only been six days since your wedding, and I should still be in Puerto Morelos, writing at my own secretaire, inspired as always by the waveless, turquoise water, and the magical music of, (what else?), "Finding Neverland" in the background. By now, you would be back from your honeymoon in Tulum, and we would be lying on the white sand, giggling and reminiscing about your magnificent wedding.

But, of course, we know why our plans changed!

At 2:00 a.m., Hurricane Emily roared into the entire Yucatan Peninsula with winds of over 150 miles an hour, and waves reaching fifteen meters. Remember a long time ago, after we experienced the earthquake in Mexico, I wrote to you how we all knew that natural disasters are imminent, but we prefer to live in denial? Denial was a luxury we didn't have this time.

Before I go into the details of the worst July hurricane in the Yucatan Peninsula, I want to share with you my thoughts and my memories about the best July wedding ever in the land of the Mayas.

The ironic part was that it was actually hurricane Dennis that worried me. I had been following its path on the computer for over a week. But it was still far away, wreaking havoc in Jamaica, so there was no need to worry you ... yet.

However, when I wasn't aware, the hotel's wedding planner did just that. She took you and Juan to the side and prepared you for the different scenarios, in case Hurricane Dennis continued to threaten Puerto Morelos. She tried to be as kind as possible as she prepared you for your options, explaining that if Dennis turned into a tropical storm, bringing with it dark skies, heavy winds and waves, you would not be able to have your wedding on the pier under the palapa. In other words, everything we had dreamed of and planned to the ultimate detail might not become a reality. The wedding would then be moved inside. Of course, this was the best possible scenario. In the worst case, the eye of the hurricane would land here in Puerto Morelos, and you would have to cancel the wedding completely, and take refuge with your guests in the shelters.

The wedding planner had just broken the news to you when I arrived at the large and rustic lobby of the hotel. I was filled with delight and pre-wedding excitement, when I spotted you sobbing, nestled in Juan's arms. Teary eyed, you blurted out to me the discouraging, possible turn of events. Juan's arms held you so strongly and tightly, it was impossible to believe anything could go wrong. His words mirrored his body language, as he lovingly reassured you that the sun would come out for you, shine on your day, and everything would go exactly as planned.

It was at that moment I fell in love with Juan, too. If, in the future he would hold you as gently, be as patient and understanding, and continue to fill you with hope and optimism, then you would always have refuge and shelter from the inevitable storms of life. "You see?" I silently said, with a mother's grateful heart, "you see my Vivi, there just might be a 'Prince Charming' after all; only today's 'princes' are defined by their integrity, consistency, and gentleness".

Juan was not only a supportive, future husband, he also turned out to be an accurate weather predictor. At the last minute, as if Hurricane Dennis succumbed to true love and knew you were getting married, it changed course and went to Cuba. Yes, indeed, another miracle!

Meanwhile, in Puerto Morelos, the three-day wedding marathon had begun. Your friends who had come from Brazil, Argentina, Germany, the United States, and Mexico had all arrived. But the first night was reserved for only your closest girlfriends and family.

At 9:00 p.m., twelve of us met at a typical Mayan hut, where we all sat on the floor on pillows in a circle. You sat on a special chair with a bowl of water at your feet, so we could all look up to you. The floor was covered with white organza, long-stemmed yellow oleanders, and twelve, tea candles in the middle.

With the soft music from "Goddess Chants" in the background, and as a symbol of humility and our love for you, each of us took turns washing and then drying your feet. Then a bowl with different shaped, tiny, beads was passed around, and we were told to chose the shape that most symbolized your essence. Each of us took turns describing the bead and you; words like unique, and strong, and giving, and beautiful were expressed. The beads would eventually be made into a necklace for you so you could remember our words and keep them close to your heart. But it was the sincerity and emotion behind the words, the admiring looks and tears that streamed down the faces of your friends as they spoke, that truly described what we felt about you, my darling Vivianne. When the ceremony ended, we each gave you one of the yellow oleanders, and with them the opportunity for a private moment.

It was late when the ceremony ended, and we all walked on the beach on the way to our respective lodgings. We grew quiet as we walked as each of us was filled with the magic of the evening. You threw each of the flowers we handed to you at our farewell into the ocean, and under the star-studded Mexican sky, as we watched, you made a wish. Your wish was silent ... but mine isn't.

May you, one day, have a child as giving and generous as you, and may she or he bestow upon you the gifts of love and pride that you give me every day of my life. Today, in the palapa, once again I witnessed the love and respect you inspire from those closest to you, and once again, I felt immense pride in my miracle child who is now a powerful, gentle, and loving woman. Once again ... a moment, a memory ... that would be imprinted in my mind forever.

"Remember, remember, remember."

Vivi, as you walk solemnly into the most challenging and intimate relationship of your life, hold this girlfriend ceremony close to you, not only as a symbol of how much you are loved, but also as a map for expanding love. The ritual in the Mayan hut was born from your friend, Paula's wonderful imagination. Our desire to show you our love in a way that fit you made us all dramatists, painters, actors, and poets.

We reached into ourselves, into our memories of being with you, and imagined an expression of our love. By the way, those memories for all of us had one thing in common; talking to you and listening to you. Like the very breath that enters and leaves our bodies is this core of listening and talking. It binds us all to you. It is you who has chosen to be a person who trusts us enough to show us your fears, your anger, your joy. It is you who has chosen to be a person who presses us gently, inquiring and discovering who we really are. It is you who has created these memories with your loving generosity, non judgmental devotion, and sage advice.

Our candles and beads and flowers thrown into the sea are no different from the kisses, caresses, and playful experimentation you and Juan will share. They mean little, in and of themselves, but endowed with the memories of your ongoing openness, they become the greatest physical, emotional, and spiritual pleasure.

The celebration continued the next night with the parrillada on the beach ... where your guests who lived on different continents reunited after years of separation. As I watched from the side, I pondered that it was like a family reunion as the tears and hugs continued to flow. The Cuban band you hired on the Internet, and with whom you spoke a dozen times, never showed up, but you handled your disappointment well, my darling, and we made our own music. We left early because lots of your guests had planned tours to take advantage of the Mayan pyramids, crystal clear cenotes, jungle kayaking, and white whale swimming that makes Quintana Roo so special and unique.

Then the day finally arrived; July 9th. Granted, the hurricane seemed to be playing games by teasing us with drizzles, but they only lasted minutes. When the time came for you and your teary-eyed father to walk down the pier, Juan was there with open arms, awaiting you under the palapa. The winds had disappeared, the rain halted, and yes, the sun came out!

The pier was decorated with bamboo torches, gigantic sea shells, organza ties that flowed in the wind, and green, ivy branches. The rafters of the palapa were wrapped with the same transparent organza and green ivy. It was just as I had envisioned months before from my bedroom window that overlooks the pier. You were like a beautiful mermaid who had ascended from the ocean; tall, statuesque, beaming with happiness.

The ceremony was like no other, because it was written just for you and Juan by your Spiritual Guide. She invoked the presence of all those whom you loved who had passed away, and explained that the Mayans had chosen this spot because it was a vortex of love and energy. She further told us that the turquoise color of the water that surrounded us ... and that you had chosen as the theme of your wedding meant unconditional love in the Mayan tradition, and that as long as you and Juan continued to share open communication and unconditional love, your lives would be blessed. She then performed a loving ritual where you and Juan physically touched each other's hearts, and said your own vows.

Still, no rain, no wind ... only lots and lots of tears. (Thank you Shalk, god of the wind and water, for controlling your forces, and giving us this splendid and heartfelt day.)

So, it was off to dreamland for your mami. I could finally sleep without worrying about the flowers, or the video, or the pictures, or lodgings, or the weather. I so looked forward to plopping into my bed, finally letting go, and being completely at peace.

But at about 6:00 a.m. I heard the sound of a loudspeaker; the loud, muffled voice ominously warned, "Alerta Amarilla! Alerta Amarilla!" ("Yellow alert! Yellow alert!")

"What in the world is a yellow alert?" I asked myself, half asleep. The voice was muffled, but it sounded serious, so still half asleep, I ran to the door and opened it. I was able to glimpse a little, beat-up, grey Volkswagen beetle with three loudspeakers propped on its old roof, turning the corner. After inquiring, I found out the muffled voice was warning everyone of a possible hurricane. "But, Dennis went to

Cuba," I thought. "Somebody better give this guy the latest weather report."

However, it was Dennis' cousin, Emily, that was threatening Quintana Roo this time, and it appeared she was determined not to be distracted. A yellow alert only meant there was a tropical storm heading our way. It was the orange and the red that we feared, because they warn of heavy rains causing possible flooding, 120 m.p.h. winds, and inevitable destruction of buildings, and possibly loss of life.

On the fourth day following the warning, I was awakened by the hammering and drilling of home owners boarding up their homes , in hopes of protecting them against the imminent rain and wind. I no longer heard the chirping of birds singing. They knew what they had to do, and had flown away.

We also knew what we had to do. So, we reluctantly agreed to close the hurricane shutters, and take the next plane for Mexico City. As we left Puerto Morelos behind, I thought to myself that we were also, symbolically, leaving my little girl behind. She was now a married woman, in control of her life and sexuality.

The rest is history. Here I am in Mexico City. As I sit here, writing to you, far from the hurricane, I am grateful we are all out of harm's way. Such destructive power ... and yet we are safe. Why? Thinking back, I remember the loudspeakers, the radio, the phone calls, and the incessant communication that flowed to us, around us, and eventually caused us to lift ourselves out of the path of danger.

I know you may roll your eyes when I say this, Vivi, but I can't help thinking that sex packs a lot of power, like a great storm. It does! It drives us, it lights us up ... if we permit it ... but it can also create deep shadows of pain and turmoil within us. Only our constant stream of communication keeps us on the safe side of that power. Only 100% honesty and communication can guide you through the powerful tides and winds of sex. Always, always say the truth. Don't hold anything in. Let Juan know what you need, what you want, and what you don't want. Don't make him guess. Don't be afraid to offend or hurt him. Telling the truth will only bring you closer together, in every way.

And the similarities keep coming to me! Hurricanes don't follow conventional rules. They are unpredictable, and can change their intensity from one minute to the next. One hurricane is never like the other. So, it is with sex. It never starts the same way twice. It never feels the same way twice. It is totally unpredictable. And that is what makes it so exciting. We can't control a hurricane. No one can tell it what to do. And so are we with our loved one; we let go, we allow for the ebb and flow of feelings, we accept the inevitable changes in intensity; we are patient; there are no expectations; it just is, and we receive its intensity. The hurricane is surrounded with mystery. How strong will it be? How long will it stay? When will it come? And it's the same with sex. How often should you have sex? What should it be like? No one knows. Since there are no rules, every experience is different.

However, there is one big difference between a hurricane and sex. Once the hurricane hits the eye, or the center, we have no control. But, when you have stepped inside that powerful sexual center, you are in control. You know what you want. You know what you like. You know how to achieve it. And you have the power to get it for yourself. You are no longer the victim of a something out there, or of the unknown. You are the owner of your destiny and your pleasure. When you are angry, know that your anger is about you and what you expect, not his failings. When you are angry, talk about yourself to Juan. Tell him about you. Sex and anger don't mix. It's like trying to ride a bicycle in the middle of a hurricane. Give it up, drop the pretense and talk about yourself, your insecurities, and your perceptions. Tell the truth. Be vulnerable. Let him see you. Then, and only then, will love play be love and play.

My darling, I dare share this with you because these are things I didn't know when I married. My whole life I was told what not to do; not to wear provocative clothes, not to let boys touch me, not to kiss on a first date. No one told me how to make the transition from being asexual to sexual. I didn't know how to become a sexually healthy woman. I thought I was supposed to be good. If I knew, if I showed an interest in sex, if I initiated, or asked for what I wanted, I was afraid I would appear to be experienced and improper.

I am aware that things are very different now, and you can talk with your sisters and friends. I just want you to know that as much as I wish for you a life of compassion, sharing, and health with Juan, I also wish for you to have an integrated life; a life where you are sexually confident, physically uninhibited, and intensely orgasmic.

So, the only question now is, when can I return to my paradise? Your personal paradise with Juan is just beginning, and mine in Puerto Morelos is still there ... possibly damaged, but waiting for me ... for us.

May you and Juan live intensely, may you continue to weather the storms of life, and always be safe and protect each other from outside (and inner) dangers.

Be happy, my darling,

Les quiero,

su mami

The What And How Of Sex

"...Most of us are like the owners of a precious
Stradivarius violin that we have never learned to play."
Jolam Chan *"The Tao of the Loving Couple"*

Celebrating Our Unique Selves

If we envision sex to be about youth or our bodies or technique or power or perfection or how we look, then we might shy away from sex as we get older, if we haven't already.   Sex, to me, is the most sublime expression of who we are beyond our physical bodies. It is a combination of spirit, earthiness, creativity, and communication. It is our opportunity to mutually show and receive love, appreciation, and abandonment. Sex is about our right to express our unique selves without restraint, without fear, without guilt. It is about honesty, and intimacy, and being true to ourselves, and not unconsciously accepting or living the sexual lives that others think we should have.

Above all, it is about freedom; freedom to delight in our bodies and feel wondrous; freedom to say no, so that our yes has more value; freedom to be all that we are, depending on the moment and the occasion ... tender and demanding, passive and proactive, conservative and adventurous, vocal and quiet, acquiescing and denying. It's about being and expressing our true selves.

The Definition and Facts

Sex is about giving and receiving sexual pleasure, and quite possibly, (and most probably), will change with each stage of life or partner.

Sex is not intercourse, but it can be. (Intercourse is only one of a number of ways to give and receive sexual pleasure.)

Sex doesn't have to include a partner. But it can. (Pleasuring yourself is one of the best and easiest ways to enjoy your body.)

Sex doesn't even have to incorporate ejaculation, orgasm, or genital touching. But it can. (Fantasy, cuddling, massaging are satisfying substitutes.)

Sex, doesn't have to become less pleasurable with age ... but it can. (Learning to take care of your sexual body and mind requires discipline and commitment.)

Sex is anything that gives you sexual pleasure, and quite possibly, (and most probably), will change with each partner. (Repetition is intended to emphasize my point of view.)

The Confusion

The woman's movement gave us permission to be equal not only in the workplace, but in the bedroom. "The Vagina Monologues", by Eve Ensler, translated into thirty-seven languages, taught us to love our vaginas. "Sex and the City" portrayed "good girls" having a lot of casual sex, and "The L Word", a cable television program, highlights lesbianism as normal and erotic. Today, almost every women's magazine graphically outlines in detail how to masturbate and achieve multiple orgasms. A reality television program from England called "Sex Research", guides you through the paces of lovemaking using infrared lighting. Dr. Ruth (and her imitators) unabashedly show us how to stimulate our clitoris and G-spot, using special props.

However, in spite of all the information about sex today, and maybe because of it, women of all ages are still confused. One minute we are instructed to "let go and just have fun", and then another, told that sex is a very serious matter. After an intimate encounter, men tell us they love us, then leave the next day, never to return. Movies and songs lead us to believe that erotic bliss is easy to achieve. Life teaches us it just ain't so.

The truth is, sex is anything but straight-forward or clear cut. It encompasses every aspect of human feeling and experience. It can be so wonderful or horrible, so natural or artificial, so fulfilling or frustrating, so life affirming or life denying, so health giving or disease activating, so graceful or clumsy, so blissfully rewarding or painfully shameful. It can bring out our best attributes and worst fears, make us feel like goddesses or tramps, elevate us to our higher selves, or descend us to our most primal selfishness.

Everything Changes

Nothing in life stays the same, and sex is no exception. As we get older, sex changes, for many reasons. On the positive side, one would presume we are finally at peace with our sexuality ; are familiar with our bodies and less self conscious; know what we like and need, and can ask for it. On the less positive side, sexual vitality and interest diminishes because of the subsiding of sex hormones; because of pent up resentments, because of illness, because of stress. It also transforms us due to the techniques of different men we have been with; because there is no one to have sex with, because we find out that we prefer women to men. Whatever the changes, (perceived as positive or negative), too often we don't understand their origin, and can come to wrong conclusions.

He is on an antidepressants or heart medication that lowers the libido. He thinks his lack of interest in sex is because she has gained weight.

She experiences pain and dryness during intercourse due to hormonal changes. She believes it's because he doesn't excite her anymore.

He has problems getting and maintaining erections because of his low levels of testosterone. He blames her, and thinks a younger lover will be the panacea.

She doesn't know that as she loses estrogen, her vagina becomes dry and her labia thins, resulting in pain. If only she knew that bio-identical hormones and a water-based lubricant would solve her problems.

He is unaware that his erectile problems can be caused by a myriad of reasons. If only he knew that men also can benefit from hormone replacement therapy (HRT) and kegel exercises.

Your Love Muscle

A strong, muscular body is attainable at any age if we stress our muscles. There is another muscle that must be used, or it too will shrink ... but this one is invisible. And although invisible, it can be more enticing to our partner than a toned body with perky breasts.

This very private, hidden muscle is found in the depth of our groins, in the pelvic floor ... the gateway to the vagina ... and its correct name is the pubococcygeal muscle, or otherwise know as the love muscle. Although very small, the exercising of this muscle will not only bring pleasure beyond our imagination, but will avoid future possible sexual relationship problems, urinary disasters, and painful bladder operations. The PC muscle exercises, commonly known as Kegel exercises, or Kegels, are easy to do. The results cannot be seen by the naked eye, but are tremendously enjoyed while naked.

The mathematics are very simple; the stronger the PC muscle, the stronger the orgasm. And since every chapter in this book is about being stronger, in one way or another, let's learn how to make our PC muscle strong through Kegels.

> I don't understand why every gynecologist doesn't tell her patients about the importance of doing Kegel exercises. No more embarrassing Pampers! No more leaking when we jump rope or we're in the middle of an intense orgasm!

To familiarize yourself with these muscles all you have to do is sit on the toilet. As the urine begins to flow, try stopping it. The muscle that stops the flow of urine is, yes, the PC muscle. Hold for one second. Release. Keep holding and releasing as many times as you can. Make sure you are not using your stomach, thigh, or buttocks muscles. After the last release, empty your bladder completely. Don't worry if you can't do it the first time. Like any other muscle, this one can also be trained to do what we want.

It is our intimate secret when, (and why), we choose to exercise it. We can work it standing, sitting, or lying down; when we are watching television, or walking down the street, or while at church. In fact, we can use it wherever and whenever we want. However, it's easy to forget to do our exercises. I do mine in the car. As soon as I put my rear end on the car seat, it triggers a message that it is "Kegel" time. Traffic and long distances all of a sudden become an opportunity for me to not only work my muscle, but also to arrive at my destination feeling very sexy.

Kegel Exercises

Kegel Exercise #1. Inhale deeply and slowly through your nose to the count of five. (Inhale from your stomach, and try not to lift your shoulders.) Hold your breath for five seconds, and at the same time squeeze your PC muscle. Slowly exhale to the same count, by blowing air through your open mouth, and release your PC muscle at the same time. Do at least two repetitions, and work up to ten.

Kegel Exercise #2. Rapidly flex and release the PC muscle as if it were a butterfly. Start with one set of ten, and little by little work your way up to two or three sets.

Kegel Exercise #3. Contract and hold the PC muscle for ten, long seconds. At the end of the count, give one, quick, deep squeeze, and then release. Relax for another ten seconds and repeat. Do as many as you like.

May I recommend getting a soft and receptive Wondrous Vulva puppet to help you understand and share how to do your Kegels. There is even a fun CD to giggle to as you break the ice with your lover. It can also be used so your children can learn to love their vaginas.

Silent Fears

With 52 million female baby boomers in their fifties, you would think we would all be talking about the sexual changes we are going through as a result of menopause. After all, the women who today are in their fifth decade of life, are the vocal generation who (thirty years ago) unabashedly banded together to fight for equality of the sexes.

But today, in the midst of menopause, we are silent, embarrassed, or in denial of the sexual changes we are experiencing. This denial, silence, and shame surrounding menopause and aging, reminds me of the shame we felt the first time we menstruated. Regardless of age, we share the memory of the dreaded tale-tale red mark, and the first time that we wore a Kotex between our legs and were sure the boys would know.

Menstruation meant we were getting older. Menopause means we're just getting old. Trust me, there is a big difference in the two. With both menopause and menstruation, we feel our bodies are betraying us. But the changes we experience with menopause have a different meaning. This time around our breasts aren't growing, they're sagging; our bodies aren't filling out, they're getting wider. This time, instead of losing baby fat, we are finding it in new places; instead of pimples that disappear later, we get permanent wrinkles and creases. This time, instead of having raging, sexual hormones that make us hot to go "all the way," all we want is for him to "get away", because we are hot, sweaty, tired, and bloated.

Quoting Sharyn Wolf , "You can't expect to be turned on by what turned you on when you were twenty. As we grow and mature, so will our sexual styles and needs. Your sex life reflects your willingness to be open to all forms of sexuality, including masturbation."

Pleasuring Ourselves

The good news is that just as we discovered puberty was not the worst thing that could happen to us, neither is menopause. In fact, as I have stated so many times, with an understanding of what is happening to our bodies and the choices that we have to remain sexy, beautiful, and fit forever, we can convert our older years into our most rewarding, fulfilling, and yes, sexiest time of our lives.

Masturbating keeps our genitals lubricated and functioning. It also tells us what we like, and what hidden desires we have locked within us. If we're having sex with a partner, it allows us to guide him more clearly.

Here are 12 Great Reasons to Masturbate:

> Whatever your age, if you do or do not want to have sex with another person, I suggest you keep your sense of self-discovery and self-care alive by masturbating regularly.

1. first step in becoming a great lover
2. makes you feel sexy
3. expands your capacity for receiving pleasure
4. puts you in touch with your body
5. strengthens your PC muscle
6. shows you how many orgasms you can have
7. relaxes and puts you to sleep
8. makes you feel powerful
9. can do it anywhere, even if you are sick
10. increases vaginal lubrication, and minimizes the discomfort of dryness
12. makes you a better lover because you know what pleases you, and you have experienced it without guilt or shame.

Here's a cute story about Clara, the woman who helps to keep my house organized and clean. She also works at an upscale, private nursing home here in La Jolla. One day, when she was doing spring cleaning at my house, Clara let out a scream because something started to move around in a bag that was hidden under my bed. She inadvertently had come across my wonderful latex vibrator, which works with batteries. Once Clara realized it wasn't some strange animal hiding under my bed, she was curious as to its purpose, since she found a similar one tucked away under the pillow of a sweet old lady in the nursing home, who was in her nineties! In fact, Clara's experience isn't as unique as we would imagine. Thirty-three percent of women over seventy masturbate regularly. (Kinsey 1995)

Single and Sexy

So many of us who are 50 + are single, sexy, and yearn to find a partner to share our lives with. However, initiating a new romance is an invitation to open Pandora's box. How do we approach our new partner-about vaginal dryness, or lack of libido? How unromantic! How embarrassing! How do we react to our new lover's problems of getting or keeping an erection? Whatever we say is wrong. This is heavy "stuff" that no one warned us about, much less prepared us to address with compassion and intelligence.

And if these new, unforeseen challenges aren't enough, there are even more hurdles to get over in order to enjoy a lifetime of pleasure. If we haven't taken care of our bodies, it is now that we are paying the consequences. Our bodies are less than perfect, and we wonder if anyone will find us attractive. If we have overly focused on our outside appearance, we are dealing with accepting the inevitable changes and must learn to love ourselves in spite of them. On still another dimension, if our identity depended upon our children who are now gone, we need to dig deep and find new interests and meaning that will provide us with the confidence needed to seek out a new partner. And last, but certainly not least, we all have to face one of the greatest fears of any age: vulnerability. Vulnerability and sex go hand and hand, and as those of us who have lived 40+ years well know, there is always the danger of being hurt ... again and again.

Most of the above fears are lived unconsciously, and are masked with excuses, like "I'm too old for sex." I bring them to the surface, because, I believe ... I know ... I insist ... we are never too old.

If you follow the advice in this book, you know you have control of your body and your mind. You can be healthy, strong, and sexy if you are willing to put in the work. Keep reading. I hope to convince you that facing the challenges of sex after 50 are more than worth the effort.

> **Sex is too wonderful, too pleasurable, too fulfilling to give up because we have to do the physical and mental work to deserve it. As in every aspect of life, we don't get something for nothing.**

The following is a very brief summary of solutions to the most common physical and emotional complaints I hear from older women. The purpose of the list is for you to be aware you are not alone ... there are solutions ... and to consult with your doctor or gynecologist. Remember, in every case, do not hide, deny, or feel ashamed.

Problem: dryness and thinning of vagina:
Solution: bio-identical estrogen, water based lubricant, local
           estrogen, Kegels

Problem: painful to have intercourse:
Solution: BHRT (Bio identical hormone replacement therapy);
           water based lubricants, different position, slower
           movements

Problem: cystitis (the honeymoon urinary disease)
Solution: urinate after intercourse, drink lots of water, take an

antibiotic before or after intercourse, stress cleanliness. (it will pass once your body gets used to having sex again.)

Problem: body image-weight gain:
Solution: focus on him instead of you; therapy, personal trainer, exercise, diet

Problem: insecurity:
Solution: same as above

Problem: lack of desire:
Solution: check hormone levels with blood or saliva test, dare to do/wear/experiment with erotica, masturbate, look for core reasons, and communicate

Different Options for Different Needs

If we are lucky enough to have a partner, and continue to enjoy sex after a lifetime together, there is probably nothing more rewarding. "We have better sex than ever! I feel so much more comfortable with my body than I did when I was younger. I don't worry about being perfect anymore. Since he (or she) is retired, we have more time, and with the children gone, we can be more creative and playful."

Even then, when we are in the throws of peri-menopause, the last thing we feel like having is sex, and we may just want to be caressed and cuddled. Blessed is the woman who is conscious of her needs, knows how to communicate them, and has a man who listens and understands!

> Sexual intercourse should never be the goal. The goal is really intimacy, communication, and pleasure, and intercourse is not necessary to achieve our objectives. If something, or a certain position doesn't work, find another way. Adapt. Have fun. Be investigators.

If your partner has arthritis or is overweight, there are certain positions you can't do. So what? There are others you can do. There is always a way to enjoy each other, as long as you have communication.

However, shared years alone, especially years without sexual fulfillment or honest communication, only predict more of the same ol' same ol'. We may have built up many reasons for anger and resentment, and use these to rationalize holding back. In fact, too often our lovemaking wasn't always that great anyhow, and now that we are older, it's a relief to not have to pretend, or go through the routine we know too well.

There are also mature couples who have decided to exclude sex completely from their everyday interactions. They say they are just fine, but in my opinion, they are losing out on thousands of moments of bliss, comfort, joy, and closeness.

Unspoken Fears

So, we have run full circle; back to the times of pretending to not know ... that we are changing, that we don't feel the way we used to, and that we don't have the vitality, reaction time, moistness, or libido that we once did. Back to the magical thinking of, "If we don't recognize it, if we don't address it, it will go away." And the it can be anything from a lump in our breast, to a lack of one in his pants, to the one in our throats that keeps us from expressing ourselves. (That's the biggest lump of all!!)

As I stated before, I know. It's not easy. We all have fears, blocks, challenges, and distractions. But these self-defeating thoughts only keep us from getting what we want; a delicious, open, creative, and loving sex life.

The Truth

Too often, the enjoyment of sex is perceived as something only for the young. Sex among seniors is even portrayed as something disgusting and unnatural. It is forbidden in most retirement homes. When Jay Leno announced Carol Channing's wedding to her 84 year old high school boyfriend, he joked, "The wedding was beautiful, but the honeymoon was disgusting." Everyone in the audience laughed. In other words, just the thought of two, older people making love makes us uncomfortable.

Stereotypes abound when, (god forbid), sex is mentioned in the same breath as older adults; dirty old man; horny old broad; the chaste, older person. All stereotypes exist to bundle people into a group, and create myths or lies about them, and when heard often enough, by enough people, (no matter how inaccurate), they become "truths". By accepting the lie that sex is only for the young, older women, (and men), are depriving themselves of one of the most important and gratifying aspects of life, not to mention their health.

> The truth is, sex has everything to do with giving and receiving pleasure, and nothing to do with age, perfect body parts, or the size of genitals. A woman's sex drive changes very little over the years. In fact, the refractory time, (the time between orgasms), does not change. A woman of sixty can have as many simultaneous and multiple orgasms as she did when she was twenty. (_The Kinsey Institute New Report On Sex_, 1995)

I, personally, am not going to give up on any part of my existence only because of a number on my drivers license, even if that number is way up there.

Good sex is ageless because it is about being willing to risk losing ourselves to passion, being vulnerable and open to intimacy, and experiencing all of the range of emotions that accompany making love. Sometimes it is harder when we are older, because we often feel less competent and useful in our lives, and no longer have a general sense of self-esteem, which will filter into our sex lives.

A Personal Story

The other day I went to the gym with my daughter, Vivianne. Vivianne is thirty-three, does yoga every day, and is 5' 8". Trust me, she looks a lot better than I. But, I was the one to get the attention.

Maybe it's because there aren't many 60+ women lifting weights, and maybe because a young man feels safe flirting with an older woman. For whatever reason, here were two, different, young men, complimenting me. So I humbly responded, "You mean, I look good for my age." I found the answer interesting for all of us who weren't born yesterday. One of the young men said, "It's more than that. It's ... it's the way you carry yourself. It's your posture." The other man said it was my smile and my enthusiasm when I talked with my daughter.

I guess it's not the same if a thirty-three-year-old puts her shoulders back and walks with confidence as when an older woman does. There's an air of mystery to solve, to try to get to know her, to find out her secrets, to learn from her, to be with her. It is my observation that men are more attracted to women who are happy and enthusiastic and express themselves with passion and intelligence, than to women with perfect breasts and rear ends. And we are a lot less threatening and more approachable.

Maybe it's because we're not worried about our biological clock, (that stopped beating a long time ago), or because we don't want to get married, (for those of us that are single), or because we're still excited about life, or because we're smart, or because we're comfortable with ourselves, that men want to be in our presence. In fact, men and women, young and old, will search us out if we can get beyond the distorted, cultural images, and stay in touch with our inner happiness.

It's Never Too Late

The first step is to be open to change the way we think about things; things like masturbation, like initiating sex, like being open to new positions, like being creative and dressing up or playing games; things like asking for what we need, like learning to talk sexy, like being vulnerable and honest; like trying new things. (There are digestible powders and oils that our breath can heat; not to mention dozens of innovative vibrators.)

It All Begins in the Brain

The question then is, why is this natural act that billions of people everywhere on the planet engage in every day, lived often with taboos, secrecy, and shame? Of course, the answer would entail complicated religious, historical, philosophical, and personal analyses ... far too complicated to address in this book. However, suffice to say, the problems begin in our brains, with the messages we have been given, not in our sexual organs. Quoting Sharyn Wolf again, "...You (must) stroke the mind before you stroke the behind, because sex begins in the brain." (*"So You Want to Get Married"*)

Have you ever wondered where your thoughts about sex come from? Better yet, have you ever considered it's your thoughts about sex that affect your sexual behavior? We live in the illusion that our thoughts and opinions are our own, but if we don't doubt and question where they came from, it's almost a certainty they originated a long, long time ago ... probably before we were five.

Do you remember who was the first person who told you how babies were born? What was the unspoken message you received? How old were you? After that, what were the messages you received from your family? Your friends? Your culture? And if you are thinking no one talked about it, then that was the loudest message of all! Wouldn't you agree?

Francesca, (Vannessa's best friend and my daughter-in-love), doesn't remember where she learned about sex, but she does remember that her mom signed a slip saying she couldn't learn about it at school. It was not only forbidden to talk about, but when watching TV with her family, even when she was eighteen, she had to close her eyes in the kissing scenes. Her dad still changes the channel if there is a kissing scene, and she is thirty-two.

Please Answer the Following Questions:

What ghosts from the past are living in your bedroom?

What ghosts from the past are wandering around in your head?

What do you have to gain by permitting the ghosts to stay alive?

What would happen if you told the ghosts to leave?

What would you specifically say if you wanted them to leave you alone?

What if you thought of the ghosts as uninvited guests?

When was the first time you received the message that your sexual thoughts were bad?

Who gave you this negative message?

How did the negative message about sex make you feel?

How do you feel about this message today?

What do you think about the messages you received today?

What do you understand today that you didn't understand yesterday?

How would you answer, today, those who gave you negative messages?

Can you say "four" letter words?

What does it feel like when you say "four letter words?

Do you know what you want from a sexual relationship? List at least 7 things you want in a sexual relationship:

1. _____
2. _____
3. _____
4. _____
5. _____
6. _____
7. _____

Can you ask for them?

Here is Linda's list:

1. I want to feel attractive ... beautiful is better, and gorgeous is the best.
2. I want to feel that my partner ENJOYS making love to me, and can also play and joke at our inevitable clumsiness and imperfect movements and body parts.
3. I want my partner to be completely there, completely into us.
4. I want my "no", and unique style of expression to be respected.
5. I want him to embrace foreplay and enjoy afterglow.
6. I want to make love in many ways that have nothing to do with sex.
7. I want him to tell me how I can please him, and for him to lovingly and patiently help me get over any hang ups I have.

Although older doesn't automatically mean wiser, nor does it necessarily mean happier, or healthier, or sexier, it can be about all those things! If we don't give up, if we don't listen to our negative self talk, if we don't limit ourselves, and if we do our work, everything ... yes, everything can and should get better. In almost all cases, the way we experience the last stage of our lives is a choice!

Ten Empowering Tips For All Ages

1. Focus on making love as a process, as if it were a wave that you ride.

2. Use all of your senses; look, smell, touch, taste, listen, laugh, and enjoy the moment.

3. Diversify. Use different positions, places, time of day.

4. Be vulnerable and intimate. Make eye contact, and let him know you celebrate what you find.

5. Forget about yourself and your defects. He really doesn't care. What he cares about is that you are enjoying his body, not thinking about yours.

6. Do something different. Try something new. Risk. Buy sexy, fun board games. Use sex toys.

7. Use candles, incense, bubbles, music, massage, sexy clothes, and costumes.

8. Exercise. It's all about irrigation and getting the blood to our sexual organs.

9. Never have expectations; then you will never be disappointed.

10. COMMUNICATE, COMMUNICATE, COMMUNICATE. Tell him your fears, your needs, and the changes you are experiencing.

Empowering Tips for
Peri- and Post-Menopause

Realize that sex and love are more precious, because we have less time to lose.

Exercise your pelvic (PC) muscle by doing kegel exercises.

Check your sex hormones through blood or saliva tests, (estrogen, testosterone, progesterone and DHEA) and, if needed, take bio-identical hormones.

Learn to be a _master_ masturbator. The best instructions are in _Bad Girl's Sex for Good Girls_, by Barbara Keesling.

Go to www.goodvibes.com for all things sexual, and for a great selection of dildos, www.a-womans-touch.com.

Read How-To sex books. Authors whose books I devour are Barbara Keesling, Laura Corn, Laurie Sue Brockway, and Sharyn Wolf.

Say your truth with compassion: "I need your help. I've been thinking about something." Or, "I'm not sure how to bring this up, but it is important . I really need your help with this one."

Forget about what you look like and focus on how good he feels and makes you feel.

Don't turn off the light to hide your sagging boobs or extra pounds. He's probably got love handles, too. It just doesn't matter. What matters is if you enjoy each other's touch.
Learn to communicate with your heart so he won't feel you are blaming him.

Go back to that time when you would drop everything and greet each other with a kiss.

Set aside alone and quality time where you can dress up, put chocolate or whipped cream on your bodies, or play creative, sex games.

Be creative; stay optimistic, playful, and up to date.

Never, never give up.

Have fun and laugh.

Think of sex like a child. It is always changing and growing, and can't survive without nourishment and care.

The Why: Benefits Of Sex

Making love not only feels good, it's also beneficial to your health. Lovemaking is great aerobic exercise as it helps circulation and works the heart. Intercourse can burn around 200 calories, the equivalent of running for thirty minutes. Endorphins released during orgasm can dull the chronic pain of backaches and arthritis, as well as migraines. Sexually active people appear to be less vulnerable to depression and suicide, perhaps because they are more comfortable with their sexuality. Hormones released during arousal can calm anxiety, ease fear, and break down inhibitions. Frequent intercourse may even boost levels of key immune cells that help fight off colds and other infections.

Early studies hint that oxytocin and the hormone DHEA, both released during orgasm, may prevent breast cancer cells from developing into tumors. Frequent orgasm has been linked to longer life; this may have something to do with sex's beneficial effects on the heart and immune system. Many ongoing scientific studies are trying to link longevity with frequent sex. "As the answers come in, the human race may begin to appreciate that the 'sex glow' stays with them a lot longer than they ever imagined." (Longevity. Org. December 2005)

In Conclusion

Only you can give the real "why". And as with all "whys", your reason to break the rules that have kept you from having a fantastic sex life will be different. I have given you my "whys"; the experience of sex is the most fulfilling of my life; it makes me feel young, passionate, alive, happy, beautiful, ecstatic. I have learned that the only limitations are in my brain. I have abandoned the limiting rules that only stifled my true sexual expression and kept me proper and frozen; I have finally given myself permission to be all that I am, enjoy parts of me I didn't know existed, and take charge of my sexual life.

> **It has taken me over six decades to understand there are no rules, no right and wrong, only freedom to enjoy, to be me. No more waiting for him to take the lead, for him to touch me, for him to make me feel good.**

I also know that everything changes and evolves, and I am just beginning to discover the wonders of my body. I invite you, in your own way, to find out there is always more to learn about your body and sexuality. I hope this chapter has at least whet your curiosity, and you will continue to investigate what works for you. Use the books I suggest at the end of the chapter, go to the web sites, experiment with the vibrators, masturbation, toys, and costumes. Sex is play, as is all of life. Play. Lose your mind, and come to your senses.

"Ultimately, if a grandfather clock stops running, your choices are junk it, fix it, or wind it up," writes Walter M. Bortz II, M.D., author of _We Love Too Short and Die Too Long_. "Aging isn't a disease. Do you feel used up? Well, you could give up. Or you could fix what's wrong and wind back up."

"This is the best time of my life –
the first eighty years are definitely the hardest."

~ Carol Channing, 82
(at her wedding reception, May 10, 2003)

Chapter Eight

Exercise
(2005)

Dearest Vanne,

How do I support you now? You live in a country where robberies and kidnappings are as common as going out for a cup of coffee, (and sometimes are even given the name "express", to refer to kidnappings that are more random and less well planned.) But, until we are confronted with an attempt against our property or our being, we have the luxury of pretending all is fine. The need for denial is sometimes necessary, because truly caring about the unconscionable acts and atrocities that happen every day, everywhere in the world, would probably drive us crazy with grief.

But, my darling, you can't deny anymore. I know that others say you were really lucky because it was just your watch. However, because you live in suppressed fear and denial, those who unwittingly judge you for overreacting don't understand your feelings. I think I do. It was the nightmare that was constantly in the back of your mind; the car closing in on you in daylight, the horrible sight of desperate thieves willing and able to take you from your safe world. It was the attack when least suspected, yet at the same time always expected, that caused your frantic screams and tears.

My first reaction, when you told me about being robbed while at a stop sign, was to tell you to get out of Mexico City and come to the United States. Sound familiar? I had the same response when we were in La Jolla and the American girls were so mean to you. However, on that occasion, I offered you the opportunity to return to Mexico. My gut feeling has always been to protect you and not let you learn your own lessons. The good thing is, I have learned since then to not, react to my first inclination. In both instances, I would be suggesting you accept injustice, and employ running away as a solution. What a bad example I was then. I hope, today, I can offer you an alternative; one that is far more powerful and empowering than running away.

Now that you and your sisters are adults, I have a new purpose, which is to look for the hidden lessons in difficult situations, and share them with you. It is because these lessons are not apparent or common, and because they are especially so difficult for me to grasp, that I dare to share them with you. They are not necessarily truths, just thoughts I am trying to put into words. And, as always, it goes without saying, you have the freedom to accept or reject them. Sometimes, like now, it takes me more time to find the lessons. But no matter how unfair, how frustrating, how devastating the situation, there is always at least one.

My Vannessa ... you who are as beautiful as a model, and as sophisticated as a debutante ... are so much deeper than what you let others see. Your real beauty shines when you work and play with your students.
I can watch you for hours and learn so much f r o m you about love and unconditional acceptance. I marvel at how you patiently convert your student's tantrums into opportunities to get closer to them and teach them lessons about life. Understanding that their acting out is actually

a cry for attention and a need to be seen, you somehow have the right words to calm them and make them smile. You give the children the most important gift of all, one that we all want and need: the gift of understanding.

So, just as you understand and convert the misbehavior of your students into opportunities, maybe one of the lessons to derive from the robbery is to understand the pain and the cry for help of the thieves that are roaming the streets of Mexico and the world. And the only way to understand the pain of others is to begin with ourselves. This concept of coming closer and accepting our pain and limitations, in order to understand others, is a practice with which I am struggling. The Buddhist premise is that if we take the time to really feel our own pain and loneliness, instead of running away from it, (by keeping busy, or shopping, or partying), we identify with the pain and despair of our sisters and brothers, who lack everything we take for granted.

It does not take a political scientist to observe that Mexican society, American society ... almost all societies ... are sick. That is why we steal, that is why we go to war, that is why there is poverty and crime. Our sickness begins in our thoughts and our feelings. And just as you are passionate about saving the planet from the disease of glut and misuse, just as you chide me when I let the water run too long in the sink, or don't separate my trash, you can also use that same energy to save the beings that live on our planet. You, and all the teachers and parents, are the only hope for the future, not only of the earth, but also of the people who live on this earth. One day you asked me, "If we continue to live like we do, what kind of world are we leaving our children?"

In your sincere endeavor to make this a better world for you and all children, you have only one challenge: to begin with yourself. You are so hard on yourself and so judgmental when you are not perfect. So, I offer you the idea of first understanding and forgiving yourself, and through that self-friendship, to continue to do exactly as you have. The difference will be an easing, a relaxation within, that eventually will become a quiet, inner smile.

When your students, and soon your children, see that you take good care of yourself, that you are happy and at peace, you will be demonstrating what unconditional love looks like.

Here is a meditation you can share with them from Thich Nhat Hanh, the well-known and revolutionary Buddhist monk who teaches love as the path to peace:

Dear little one, let us sit very quietly.
Listen ... Listen to the wind.
Listen to the birds.
Listen very quietly to your breathing.

Let us put our hand on our tummy and
feel our breathing.
Our tummy goes out and then it
goes in.
Breathing in and breathing out.
Our tummy goes out and then it
goes in.
Breathing in and breathing out.
I close my eyes and stay with my
breathing in.
I close my eyes and stay with my
breathing out.
It is so wonderful to feel my breath
coming in.
It is so wonderful to feel my breath
coming out.
Breathing in, I calm my whole body.
Breathing out, my whole body is calm.
Body, calm.
I see that my classmates and my
teacher make me happy.
We listen and we see that all life is
breathing with us

Then, when they open their eyes, ask them how they feel.
Don't be surprised if they say that all of a sudden everything
looks brighter and happier.

According to Buddhist philosophy, all living things are interconnected. When we can learn to appreciate we are all the same, we will also be able to identify with the "they" people ... the thieves, those filthy, hungry, messy strangers. And if we are they, and they are us, then there will be no need for people to steal or kidnap, and we will finally live in peace. Too simplistic? I don't think so.

If it is true that the basis for happiness is to feel understood, then our pain, our frustration, our sadness, also have to be understood in order for us to be happy. Do you think the thieves, not only those that assaulted you, but all of the thieves, the drug addicts, the kidnappers, feel understood by their societies, or by their families for that matter? Just as you open your arms to your students and make them feel understood, please offer yourself that same unconditional understanding and then offer it to everyone ... including the thieves who stole your watch and your sleep.

The truth is, we are part of a privileged class. We live with the comforts and luxuries most Mexicans cannot imagine. It is our responsibility to address the social and economic issues that actually create the turmoil we hate so much. By telling our truth ... by sharing our insights ... we can change the injustices. We do not have time to deny or feel our pain in private anymore. We have to reveal ourselves and join with others who feel the same way. It would be easy to just run away, but I have taught you since you were little to live a life of service to others.

Dear Vanne, every day I wake up an hour early and get out of bed, I want to stay in it. Every time I put on my workout clothes and drive to the gym to lift weights, I would rather be writing or reading or doing just about anything else. But, there are lessons in the gym that teach me about myself. Physical strength can help us handle difficult situations. If we can sit with the discomfort of a weight on our chest, we also can learn to sit while we are meditating and learn that we are capable of more than we thought. If we throw the weights away and give up just as we get slightly uncomfortable, could it be that we do the same in other circumstances when life gets tough? Here, with my weights in hand, I learn to endure when things get tough, and go beyond my perceived limitations; no spoiled tantrums because I want my way, no complaining, no making excuses.

I'm saying all of this to you, my strong-willed daughter, because I want you to look beyond your personal discomfort and realize, for every prick of terror, loss, and anger that you feel, hundreds of thousands of Mexicans feel stabbing wounds. This suffering cannot be alleviated by government action alone. As individuals, we must assume responsibility and lend our efforts and our hearts to the work of ending human suffering and building human solidarity.

Our body is our temple, and we are our country. In each case, we cannot leave the work to anyone else. If you want Mexico to become a safer place to live, you must actually sit down and write letters, read, and speak out. Simply complaining and leaving makes about as much sense as my wishing I were thinner before turning over and going back to sleep.

Forgive me for going on like this. What is important is that you know my heart is with you, and if I could do anything, I would take the next plane to be by your side. But it's not my place anymore. There is nothing I want more than to have you and my future grandchildren close to Vivianne and me in the United States. Yet, I have to say in truth, each country has its own shame, its own poverty, its own injustices to work on; United States being no exception. Our work is set out for us wherever we go. Running away instead of using our minds and hearts to make a difference, never has, and never will be a solution.

You and Aureo are talking about moving. Aureo needs time to weigh all the pros and cons. It takes a strong man to risk the status quo and leave all that he knows. Mexico is where he has worked so hard to make a name for himself as a music producer. (Who hasn't heard, at least in the Spanish speaking world, of the music of "Sin Bandera," "ha-ash" or "Alejandro Fernandez"?) We all think he would be successful in the Latin market anywhere, but I can certainly understand his reluctance to leave the fame and success he now enjoys.

Please know I marvel at how far you have come, at how your love for your husband has given you qualities that I didn't know in you ... such as flexibility, and patience. Love can bring out qualities in us that we aren't aware we have. But it can't bring out something that wasn't always there, and the transformation can only help with our willingness to grow and change. Let's make that one of our goals: to search for all of the dormant, ennobling qualities we possess, and bring them to the surface. And what if it is through tragedies like the one you experienced, that we can discover these ennobling qualities? We just might have to be grateful for the experience and perceive it as a gift!

Just a thought ... and very likely my timing is bad. It's probably too early for you to want to entertain the idea of your frightening experience as a gift or an opportunity for another lesson. First you need to understand your fear, grieve the loss of safety, and then there will be time for the lessons. My beautiful and loving Vannessa, I have no doubt that through the mutual love and special communication you share with Aureo, you will come up with the most loving solution for both of you.

Meanwhile, as always, know in your heart that if for any reason I can help, or if you just want me there for whatever reason, like the song says, "just pick up the phone, and I'll be there."

With you always,

tu mami que te adora

The What and How of Exercise
Resistance Training: Learning To Flex Our Muscles

We have about 605 muscles in our body. Each muscle is made up of many fibers. When we lift weights, the fibers thicken, which in turn cause the muscles to get stronger and larger. Only those fibers (not one more or one less) that are needed will be used. So, we don't lose muscle tone because we age; we age because we lose muscle tone.

Being sedentary tells our fibers we do not need them to perform. In turn, they will not grow.

> In order for our muscles to grow we must stress them. It's as if they have a mind of their own. If you make demands on them, they will meet them. If you need them more, and in different ways, they will be there to support you. If you don't, and make no demands on them, they will weaken and atrophy with age.

For me, of all the life-changing habits in my book that empower us to stay young forever, resistance training is the most important for our bodies. The discipline of lifting weights is not about chiseled bodies, ripped abs, striving for perfection, or achieving an impossible ideal. It's certainly not about our negative obsessions with our inner thighs or flaccid underarms, or looking and acting like a man.

Resistance training is about self-esteem and being empowered to fend for and take care of ourselves. And never forget, it is the number one deterrent to osteoporosis, the thinning of the bones that causes falls and debilitating injuries as we age. It is a cruel twist of fate that women who have been the personification of inner strength and power, women who, during their young years, had the stamina to work simultaneously at two jobs, nurture, nurse, and chauffeur their children, clean a house, and then take care of their husbands and aging parents, should end their days bent over and deformed due to this silent killer called osteoporosis.

Here are enough "whys" for all of us to practice resistance training:

Unused muscles shrink about ten percent each decade.

Consistent use of weights will prevent or delay hip fractures, mental deterioration, and diabetes.

We continue to burn fat after the session is over (not true of aerobic training).

Since pumping iron reduces fat, it also lowers the chances of contracting diseases such as cancer, diabetes, and heart attack.

Muscle training improves posture, especially weak lower backs, protruding abs, and humped-over shoulders.

Weight training adds density to bones, and is the only physical exercise that can prevent bone thinning.

Weight lifting can help reduce depression and insomnia.

Weight lifting improves sexual performance, self-esteem, and balance.

Weight lifting increases the Basal Metabolic Rate (BMR), the measure of calories our body uses while at rest.

For every one pound of muscle growth, you increase your BMR fifty calories a day.

Strong muscles burn more calories, even when you are doing nothing.

If all the above don't convince you, I promise you, of all the disciplines that slow down the aging process, weight lifting will provide the quickest results. The visible proof of looking more attractive and feeling stronger is a great motivator, and I am hoping that you, like I, will never want to go back to feeling weak or powerless.

One of the best kept secrets, (which is not a secret at all), is that our bodies do not have to be prisons of the degenerative diseases of aging. If I was able to open my prison door, so can anyone.

Stretching

In her workbook, "The Pilates Body", Brooke Silver talks about stretching.

She says, "I suggest yoga. Yoga uses our own body weight to build muscle but also hones flexibility and balance. However, you can hurt yourself with yoga as easily as any other exercise. So, start off slowly and take a few classes before you use a video. Pilates, which also focuses on stretching and building core body strength, is another option."

Pilates, a combination of stretching and strengthening exercises using the deepest muscles in the body, was developed over ninety years ago by Joseph Pilates. Joseph Pilates believed that in order to achieve happiness, it is important to gain mastery of our bodies and our minds simultaneously. He said, "If at the age of thirty you are stiff and out of shape, then you are 'old'. If at sixty you are supple and strong, then you are young." He believed our stress and fatigue come from poor posture, imbalances in our body, and lack of correct breathing. Pilates is more than exercise; it is an ideal life-style, attained only through balance of the physical, mental, and spiritual.

One of the main characteristics of Pilates is that it is holistic. Each movement serves a function and focuses on only one precise, perfectly executed movement. The principles of this practice are fluidity, precision, breath, imagination, and integration. Using the movements as a catalyst for engaging our minds is at the heart of our workout. For example, if we visualize a string that is pulling us at the top of our heads, or "walking on air," we have used muscles we probably never exerted before. By creating a visual image within our minds, the body is able to respond.

I prefer mat work to the contraptions with springs because it is more practical, and involves a lot less money. By training our bodies without these props, we can re-teach ourselves correct form and movement that will stay with us for a lifetime.

Aerobic Exercise

Here are some different exercises and activities that increase your blood flow, and strengthen your heart muscle:

Sailing does wonders for developing upper body strength.

Rock climbing or scrambling (a cross between rock climbing and hiking) offer full body workouts, since you use both your arms and legs.

Bouldering, a lateral version of rock climbing, is a new option. All of these sports burn over 350 calories per half hour.

Golf. If you love to kibitz and are social, then golf is your game, but it won't give you maximum toning and calorie burning. (Only about 145 calories each half hour, if you walk and carry your own clubs).

Swimming. If you are a loner, swimming is for you. It's a great total-body workout that builds stamina, and burns about 250 calories per half hour, with almost no risk of injury.

Running. Of course, running is a great endurance sport that tones the legs, abs, and upper body; it burns a whopping 300 calories per half hour.

Walking. We all know how to do. Try power walking or going uphill. Normal walking will burn 170 calories in a half hour.

Cycling is great for the lower body, but I don't like bending over, so I had an old fashioned handlebar modified for my bike.

It's Never Too Late

Everyone I know has two ages: the one that is on their driver's license, (chronological age), and the one that they look and feel (biological age); the latter is usually ten years younger than the former. At a recent dinner with my fifty-plus best girlfriends, we calculated our inner age at about thirty-five. Well, maybe we don't look thirty-five, but we certainly don't look like our mothers did at our ages. One of the main reasons we look and feel so good is that we all do aerobic exercise.

It's taken us a while to find what we like to do, and commit doing it three to five times a week for a half hour. Some of us race walk, others cycle and swim, and still others prefer going to the gym and taking their favorite aerobic classes.

The secret is to do something that you like, because if not, you eventually will stop doing it. It's never too late to start!! If you are reading this and you are close to seventy or even eighty and you have never really exercised in your life, start now! You can push back the clock. You can regain lost health.

And listen to this. According to the British Journal of Sports Medicine, men and women over fifty may get not only better with age, but also faster. Researchers found New York City Marathon runners over fifty have improved their running times significantly more during the last two decades than their younger counterparts, and older women may be outpacing the men in terms of both participation and improvement ... the biggest improvement in running time of over 14,000 female runners was seen in women aged sixty to sixty-nine.

I think the reason for this improvement is that those of us who recently have begun to exercise know firsthand how we felt, looked, and lived before we started to exercise. The difference between an older person who exercises and one who doesn't is glaring. Younger people all seem to have more or less the same amount of energy. Although they should, they don't have to exercise to complete their daily functions competently.

As we age, it's not a matter of should, but "must", if we want to continue to do enjoy our lives and do the activities we love. The swimmer or runner or walker has control over her life, is independent, energetic, and positive until she takes her last breath. The sedentary counterpart is most likely heading eventually for a wheelchair, a heart attack, pulmonary restrictions, and a life of dependence.

When we were children our parents and schools were in charge of our physical activities, so we didn't give the importance of movement a lot of thought. As young adults, we should do some sort of exercise every day; if not, we probably will gain weight, have sleeping problems, or experience a loss of energy. After forty we must exercise. If not, the consequences are life threatening. Dementia, strokes, high blood pressure, hypertension, obesity, and hip fractures often occur to older adults who are sedentary.

Aerobic activities, such as running, race walking, cycling, or swimming build overall endurance and provide significant benefits to our heart and lungs. The function of the heart is intimately connected to the function of the rest of the circulatory system.

A number of sophisticated tests can measure the overall health of the cardiovascular system. Researchers at Johns Hopkins performed these tests on a group of sixteen, high performance athletes, (average age sixty-three), and compared them to thirty-five, untrained men of similar ages. Peak oxygen consumption (the ability of the tissues in the body to take the oxygen they need from the circulation) was fifty percent better in the athletes. Cardia index, a reflection of the heart's pumping strength, was twenty-two percent higher in the athletes.

Even the very old, (age ninety and above), respond to exercise with a marked and rapid improvement in fitness and function. Staying fit will slow the functional decline common with aging, like loss of muscle strength, and can actually reverse the loss of physical capacity. The overall death rate is three times higher for those are sedentary, compared to those who are fit.

However, I believe one of the reasons I got Graves Disease was because I overextended myself at the gym, so I questioned my dear friend, Mitch Thrower, (thirteen-time Ironman competitor, owner of Triathlete Magazine, co-founder of Active.com, and bestselling author of, "The Attention-Deficit Workplace"), about excessive exercise after fifty. It is worthwhile to read his answer to me:

"Linda,

I've seen and read quite a bit about how endurance athletics tears you down, and also, counter to that philosophy, I've seen and read how it builds you up, strengthens your mind, body, soul, spirit, and energy.

There is no question that some people don't "train" smart and don't treat their bodies well in life, and the same is true with exercise. I do think that there is a way to be a healthy adult and ways to be a healthy endurance athlete. The body is amazingly resilient and responds to our requests upon it. I have always said that the fountain of youth is movement; in fact they quoted me for that in a newspaper! And I think it's true, motion leads to motion."

While the message is clear, it's not getting through to the majority of us. Only six percent of people over sixty met the national objectives for engaging in both physical activity and strength training, according to a survey published by the U.S. Centers for Disease Control and Prevention. As a nation, we become unhealthier, fatter, sicker, and more depressed, and diseases like diabetes and hypertension that were once only disabilities of the old, are now shared with children.

The Why Of Exercise

By improving blood flow, exercise keeps our heart healthy by keeping our arteries open and bringing oxygen and nutrients to our brain so it may continue to function well. At the same time,, aerobic exercise lowers cortisol (the stress hormone), increases serotonin to avoid depression, and augments the chemicals that nourish brain cells.

Countless research confirms regular exercise will help us live longer and reduce our chances of dying prematurely or acquiring disease or disability. But we need not run marathons to benefit.

By simply walking rapidly four or more times a week for thirty minutes, we can turn our biological clock back about ten years in terms of cardiovascular and aerobic function, according to "Aging With Grace", by David Snowdon. You need to do enough exercise to burn approximately 1,000 calories per week to obtain health benefits, and reduce your risk of disease.

In general, with increasing age we develop arteriosclerosis ... hardening of the arteries. Stiff arteries cannot open up or dilate adequately when challenged to do so to satisfy increased oxygen needs. Swedish researchers compared nine master athletes with an average age of seventy-five, to eleven, sedentary but healthy adults. The athletes were found to have more flexible arteries than the non-athletes. A study at the Washington University School of Medicine in St. Louis, comparing ten endurance trained men to ten sedentary men also found the athletes had more flexible arteries. Moreover, their flexibility was found in untrained muscle groups as well as trained ones.

When our muscles are stronger, our metabolism works harder and faster, which lowers body fat. Karen Andes, in, "A Woman's Book of Strength" says, "Without even moderate muscle strength, our skeletons sag, our posture crumples, and therefore our stature tumbles as well. Over time, as muscles get weak, our bones weaken too." Then, if we haven't taken care of our bones, when menopause arrives, the lack of estrogen and calcium can lead to osteoporosis. Why settle for being weak and bent over when we can do something about it?

Remember the What, How and Why triangle. The What and How you can get in books, but the Why has to come from down deep inside you. To paraphrase Nietzche: "If the Why is strong enough, any How or What are possible."

Looking For Your Own Why

Answer the following:

Why do you want to be fit?
Could you convince me?
Could I talk you out of it?
Could you talk you out of it?

Are you willing to give up certain pleasures to achieve your goal?
How many powerful reasons can you give me to do what must be done?
Will your answer sustain you when nothing else does?

These lines are provided so you can write your Why. Be honest with yourself!

_____

_____

_____

Often, the real "Why" is buried under what sounds good to you. But it doesn't matter if your reason is noble or intellectual or appealing. All that matters is that it is your Why and that it is strong enough to motivate you to do what you must.

Here are a few Whys of some amazing, energetic, positive people I know.

"Why not?"
"Because I don't want to be like those other old guys" (said to me by an eighty-eight-year-old cyclist).
"Because I feel so good for the first time in my life."
"Because my children are proud of me."
"Because I am proud of me."
"Because everyone in my family died before they were fifty, and I am in my forties."
"Because I was told that I couldn't."
"Because dying sucks."

You see, none of them are very special, though some are very funny. What is important is that their Whys are strong enough to get them to do what is necessary. And it's obviously working, because all these answers came from Senior Olympians I interviewed.

Personally, I know what the alternative to not exercising feels like, and I never want to go there again. Before I knew that my debilitating symptoms were from Graves Disease, my diagnosis for myself was "Old Age-itis."

Though billions of neurons do begin to die when we are in our forties, each brain cell has branches that reach out to other brain cells to make memory connections. As we age, our brain cells grow more and more branches, just as a growing tree keeps sprouting branches.

> By middle age, we have far more branches than we did in our younger years. Those extra branches compensate powerfully for brain cell death. Compared with the brain of a young person, ours has an almost limitless horizon. This is why we become wise with time. It's the Use It or Lose It principle at its best. The brain can change at any age. The more we think, the bigger our brains become and the better they work.

When I refer to thinking and using our brain, I mean in new ways. If you hate to memorize, then memorize (preferably something that is useful to you). If you don't like to deal with numbers, begin to challenge yourself with accounting skills. If you are sure you are right about something, study the other point of view. If you are computer illiterate, (like I am), or hate to do puzzles or play cards, (like I do), that's what you must do to create new dendrite connections. (Dendrites are the neurons that send messages to all the cells of your body.)

When Einstein's brain was dissected, at first the doctors were surprised it was no different than other intelligent men of his age. Then they discovered something very interesting. Einstein had more of a certain type of cell (glial cell) in one special area of the neocortex known as Area 39. This is the part of the brain that is used for creativity, memory, attention, and self-awareness. Although Einstein was born with a good brain, he was not born a genius. The difference between Einstein and other intelligent men was ... you got it ... he used his brain as if he were a mental triathlete!

Mental Exercises

A. Multiple associations
B. Learning new and different tasks
C. Reading the newspaper
D. Using the computer
E. Board games like Scrabble or Jeopardy

All of the above physically improve your brain, thus improving memory and mental clarity, and slowing down degenerative diseases such as Alzheimer's.

Physical Exercise

Physical exercise is as important to our brains as it is to our bodies. Did you know that twenty-five percent of the blood that circulates in our body is destined to nourish our brains? By exercising, you are pumping more blood into your brain, and giving it the nourishment it needs.

Below is a partial list of how physical exercise benefits your brain. You might not be sure what some of the terminology means. I invite you to take this opportunity to use your brain and learn something new and begin forming new dendrites to communicate with our neurotransmitters.

In terms of the brain, physical exercise:

Reduces stress hormones and increases chemicals that nourish brain cells
Improves blood flow bringing the brain oxygen
Supplies the brain with a nerve growth factor
Enhances neuronal metabolism
Increases the oxygen and glucose to the brain
Expedites the removal of necrotic debris from brain cells
Tones some neurotransmitter systems
Increases the output of norepinephrine and dopamine
Increases the availability of brain-related enzymes, such as coenzyme Q10
Decreases low-density lypoprotein
Decreases depression
Lowers blood pressure
Helps stabilize blood sugar levels

There are some things in life we have no control over. However, staying limber, strong, lean, and well toned is within our reach.

In this chapter I have mainly addressed women in the second half of their life. But ... I must emphasize ... the advice is true for all women. If you are in your twenties or thirties, and begin to exercise today, and continue throughout your life, I promise you, you will stay young forever. Remember, it's never too early or too late to begin. Please don't put it off. The time to make sure you remain healthy throughout your life begins today!

"Love does not consist in gazing at each other,
but in looking outward together in the same direction."

~ Antoine de Saint-Exupery

Chapter Nine

Love
(December 03, 2005)

Dear Vannessa, Vivianne and Jenny,

I'm sorry for not writing sooner. But, I'm here! Here in Puerto Morelos!

Puerto Morelos survived Hurricane Wilma, and so did I. My beloved fishing village and I, each in our way, were forced to relinquish our innocence and go inward. No more pretending it couldn't happen here. No more wanting to believe nature's wrath would spare us.

It took the worst hurricane in recorded history to bring us to the best place possible, a place where we have no other choice than to face the truth; a space where we can learn from our mistakes and begin anew, never to take nature for granted again; a time to pull together as one and recreate a multi-cultural sanctuary for people from all corners of the world. Puerto Morelos has always been a non judgmental and magical vortex, where those of us who are blessed to live here are accepted as the unique and special beings we are. And now, we have a chance to respect our land in the same way we do our spirits. If we can accomplish this challenge, we will eventually be stronger and more beautiful than ever.

This peaceful fishing village and I know that feeling sorry for ourselves and waiting for some external being or force to make us strong again are not options. We know that we have to be completely honest as we evaluate which areas of the destruction were inevitable, and which ones could have been avoided.

When you are attacked by 140 mile per hour winds from all sides, and an unrelenting rain that pummels everything in sight for fifty-five hours, destruction is inevitable. After surviving such devastating damage, we must humbly accept the unrestrained power of nature. Yet, at the same time, we are required to take responsibility for building on dunes too close to the ocean, erecting inadequate sea walls, and using poor grade construction materials. In each of these cases, we must be accountable and not repeat the same mistakes. No excuses. No procrastination. Just action!

Knowing the difference between gracefully accepting the inevitable and proactively creating change are aptitudes that will make the difference between our being empowered survivors, or powerless victims. (Remember the three "A's" of the book, "Working Out, Working Within"? Accept, Assess, Action!) Here, in Puerto Morelos, we are in the processes of assessing, and we have all agreed to take the necessary action.

My beautiful daughters, it is tempting for me to have you believe that these insights and determinations were just natural outcomes of my innate wisdom and confident personality. But the truth is, it took excruciating inner work for me to get to the peaceful and knowing place I share with you today. So to even suggest I had automatically and naturally arrived at this place of peace and determination would just be my ego wanting to be seen as enlightened. Tempting, but the truth is quite the contrary.

Sharing my flaws and weaknesses with you has always been my way of giving you permission to experience your own limitations, and at the same time, sharing with you the tools I use to dig myself out of holes I create.

When I arrived at Puerto Morelos five days ago, everything was just as I had seen on the Internet. Tall buildings were shrunken into unrecognizable slabs of cement; gigantic palm trees had fallen on and smashed a number of thankfully, unoccupied cars; fishing boats, speed boats, yachts were piled on top of each other in the lagoon; puddles of putrid brown water, covered the beach as long as you could see; the once lush swamp land was now just masses of barked-stripped yellow twigs and branches.

But, looking at generic pictures, no matter how devastating, didn't prepare me for the impact of reality, nor for the pain of my friends as they relived their individual horror stories of fifty-five hours of hell and anguish; much less for the almost total destruction of "our" beloved hotel Ceiba del Mar and its pier, where you and Juan took your vows only five months ago.

When I saw all of this ruin, I wanted to literally run away, go back home ... but I had no home to go back to. I had sold the house I loved to be congruent with my beliefs. I was walking my talk, practicing what I preached about expanding one's comfort zone. Remember? "Jump and the joy will follow! Go into the unknown with a sense of adventure! Don't be afraid! Risk! Improvise!"

The response from my caustic and accusing inner voice to these optimistic exclamations was an incessant and judgmental: "Blah, blah blah. How can you prefer hurricane devastated Puerto Morelos to the safety and beauty of La Jolla? Who do you think you are? The Survivor? Since when are you so adventurous? What are you going to do now? Where are you going to go? What do you think you're doing? What are you trying to prove? And why, why did you do it?"

On and on, my negative inner conversation was relentless; no matter how much I tried, I couldn't stop it from hounding me. "Life is not a fairy tale," it continued. "Did you picture little dwarfs happily singing 'whistle while you work', and you would come along like Snow White to make everything perfect?" What did you expect after the hurricane of the century?" The accusations wouldn't stop. "Did you expect everyone to be singing and dancing in the streets like in a musical, as they carried cement, hauled the blocks that once were houses, and moved the fallen trees? And don't forget, I warned you that leaving your home would be hard, but you acted without thinking ... all that 'jumping' and 'risking' stuff. Now look where you are!"

I felt powerless over her sarcasm ... and thought she was here to stay. Worst of all, I feared she was right! I didn't feel joyful, or young, or adventurous. I only felt tired, afraid, lonely, and homeless. I missed my dogs, and I had bronchitis.

After three days of chastising myself for just about every decision I had ever made in my life, I finally came to the point where I had to make a choice. I could give away my power by feeling sorry for myself and turn into the old bitter woman I had worked so hard to avoid becoming, or I could reclaim and use the power of my words in the direction of love and compassion. I decided to pull myself up by the hair and tell that voice to just SHUT UP!

However, it would have been more difficult without the love and support of Eva, my best friend of almost twenty years, who reminded me of life's cycles as she listened, empathized, and even justified my fears.

After listening to my fears, she wouldn't let me be alone, and insisted I return with her to her house. Her affectionate children received me with their usual heartfelt hugs, and shared with me how their mutual support and love kept them intact during the endless hours of darkness and pounding winds.

I was hearing how they converted a tragedy into an opportunity to work as a team and help each other. They were confirming and reminding me of the strength of the human spirit.

At the same time, there were phone calls of encouragement from my friends I left in the United States, reminding me of my true power and my ability to overcome obstacles.

There was even a new friend who promised to surround me with fairy dust to protect me when I became overwhelmed. And eventually, it was the pure presence of the men and women who had lost everything, that made me understand why I was here.

These indomitable and courageous men and women, who were grateful just to be alive and have each other, chased away my doubts and fears, and heightened my commitment to be a part of the changes.

I have a unique album in my possession of the hurricane seen through the articles and pictures of Qunitana Roo newspapers. It was given to me by Didier Briceno, the principal of the David Alfaro Siquieros Grammar School, and a soul sister who had the need to document what she lived and felt.

Perhaps you are tired of hurricane stories, but in a world where we forget so easily, I thought it was worthwhile to transcribe her letter. I hope to be able to introduce her to you the next time that you visit. I know that you too will appreciate her loving energy and determination to "assess, accept, and take action. It kind of sums up the essence of the community I live in.

November 10, 2005

"In my forty five years, I remember having lived through many hurricanes. My parents, brought us up in Chetumal, and being just a child, I remember vividly the attack of the cyclone, "Carmen" where we lost most of our land. Then I lived through others such as Gilberto, Opal, Roxana, Emily, and more whose names don't come to mind. But I can say that none were like Wilma, maybe because of the fear of so many hours of anguish in our shelter, wondering if it would ever pass and if we would be alive to tell about it. It felt like a nightmare, watching how the water rose minute after minute, no matter how much we bailed it out; hearing how the deafening howling of the wind tore out windows, doors, concrete walls, electric posts, and all the time, my family in the dark, holding hands, held high in prayer to the Almighty God and devotees of San Judas Tadeo. The hours passed, and we without knowing anything from the outside world: just the terrible noise from a tower that almost fell over us, the cries of my daughters, the face of my husband, trying to give me courage, though I could see how worried he was. All these feelings; the flavor of death, the atmosphere smelled of destruction, sadness, anguish, desperation. I have no words to express the great pain of the 55 hours we lived.

Wilma left some of us without a home, without
work, without food ... but the human values which
are in each and every one of us and the solidarity
of all the Mexicans will achieve the recuperation and
reconstruction of what was lost, giving us once again
the joy and the strength to begin again TODAY."

Didier, Eva, my friends, all offered me
LOVE; unconditional, non judgmental
love. It was love that was the sword
that combated my inner demons. Yes,
self love comes first, but when that
negative little voice is out to get us,
one way to exorcize her is with the
presence of those whose compassion
will remind us of who we really are.
And it was, and is, that love that has
brought me to the peaceful and grateful
place where I am now.

Let me quote again, Don Miguel Ruiz, "The human mind
is like a fertile ground where seeds are continually being
planted. When you are impeccable (compassionate) with
your word, your mind is no longer fertile ground for the
words that come from fear: your mind is only fertile for the
words that come from love."

So, my darlings, now I choose to see what is being done, not what still needs to be repaired; what is being rebuilt, not what was destroyed; the new green leaves that are coming back, instead of the trees that were destroyed.

You would be so proud to see everyone working together. Hundreds, maybe thousands of dedicated construction workers, masons, carpenters, and home owners are painstakingly hammering, digging, sawing, drilling, measuring, excavating, painting, planting, removing, filling in, and draining so we can return to our former lives.

Although it is almost impossible that the eye of the biggest hurricane in recorded history will attack Puerto Morelos again, we now know its potential, and how to protect ourselves. Pillars that go deep into the ground, strong, stone walls, and new construction parameters are being utilized. As for me, I will consciously plant deep into my soul the spirited acts and faces of the families that surround me, and in the future, use their courageous words to counter my internal, judgmental voice that was out to get me.

The next time you come, you will be amazed at how we have not only recovered, but are stronger and more beautiful ... kind of like the lessons of aging. Time and experience teach us what youth and innocence can never know. Right?

Let's make plans to spend New Years Eve of 2007 in Puerto Morelos, when Hurricane Wilma will just be a memory, and a reminder that anything is possible with love, commitment, and perseverance.

I love you. I love you. I love you.

your adventurous and strong,

mami

The What and How of Love

If you look up "definition of love" on the internet, you will find 42,600,000 definitions. It is defined scientifically, culturally, philosophically, psychologically, and religiously. "Love is an emotion of deep affection or devotion;" "It is the highest, deepest, and most powerful state of consciousness" "Love contains the potential of all possibility." "Love is God. God is love." "Love is timeless, changeless, formless, and eternal. "Love is a cohesive power of attraction throughout the universe."

Just about everyone has an opinion of what love is. Some believe it to be the reason we are alive, others see it as a way to get closer to God, still others are more cynical. For example, the poet, Robert Browning, declares; "Take away love and our earth is a tomb". Victor Hugo agrees: "The greatest happiness in life is the conviction that we are loved, loved for ourselves, or rather loved in spite of ourselves." Albert Schweitzer, philosopher and theologian, predictably believes, "Only through love can we obtain communion with God." German speaking writer, Franz Kafka, is more practical than his usual negative self: "Love is as unproblematic as a vehicle. The only problems are the drivers, the passengers and the road." And yes, there are the cynics like Harlen Ellison, the cartoonist, who entitled his book: "Love ain't nothing but sex misspelled" And we should note, movie producer Woody Allen's astute observation: "Sex without love is an empty experience, but as empty experiences go, it's one of the best."

Neuroscientists explain love as simply the presence of certain chemicals in the brain: testosterone, serotonin and oxytocin being the main causes of the euphoria we call love. Yes, but what activates those hormones? We don't produce them for everyone. Recently, Italian scientists discovered a molecule called

Nerve Growth Hormone, (NGH), which they attribute to the ecstatic "falling in love" experience. They add that NGH only lasts between twelve and twenty four months. Yet, there are those rare couples we admire as they lovingly walk hand and hand after 60 years of marriage, and still report being in love. Apparently there is more to their devotion than a growth hormone.

There are not only a myriad of definitions of love, there are almost as many kinds of love. According to Wikipedia, (the free, online encyclopedia), there is: agape love (universal), erotic love (sexual attraction), familial love (kinship connections), free love (open, no restriction), platonic love (close relationship without sex), puppy love (immature, unreal), religious love (devotion to a deity or theology), romantic love (affection characterized by emotional intimacy and sexual desire), unconditional (without motive or demands), instantaneous love (love at first sight), and sacrificial love (giving up our well being for a greater cause or person).

Sometimes it is easier to define what love is not than what love is. Love is not being separate from others; love is not about feeling superior or better, nor is it harmful or mean, selfish or self serving, resentful or possessive. Love is not about narcissism or ego; it doesn't demand, take, belittle, or diminish.

However, maybe we don't need to define it, since there is no mistaking it exists. We feel it in our hearts. It sooths us when we are in pain; it protects us against the storms and our enemies; it guides us when we are lost; it gives meaning to our lives. Even water knows it exists, as the amazing photographs taken by researcher Masaru Emotu, have demonstrated. When words of love, and even loving thoughts, were sent to water and then frozen, the water crystallized into beautiful intricate forms. When hateful words or thoughts were spoken, the crystals were distorted, bent, malformed, and twisted.

My perspective on love is that it simply is. We don't
have to seek it out, or look for it anywhere or in anyone.
It is already in us. All we have to do is acknowledge it's
there. It is ironic we waste so much time looking outside
of ourselves, when love is already there, inside us.

More than a feeling, love is a way of being, a spiritual
practice that we can offer to everyone and everything in
our lives. And every time we offer it we grow, we expand,
we stretch. As Khahil Gibran says in The Prophet, "Love
gives naught but itself and takes naught but from itself,
love possesses not nor would it be possessed. For love is
sufficient unto love."

And if we are very lucky, we just might find another person who
resonates with our heart, and together we could have the unique
opportunity to become more than two by offering our love to
better the world. If this miraculous soul encounter does find us,
then we have to decide if we are willing to pay the high price of
this precious gift.

The gift of true love is expensive, because it is valuable and
rare. It requires spending one hundred percent of our emotional
bank account on being vulnerable, honest, transparent, and
present, without knowing if the other will make the same
investment. We can't hold anything back. We can't even
pretend, because love will know. There is no in between, no
"mas o menos", no if's or sometimes or maybe's. And since
love isn't always bilateral, we have to be willing and open
to experience pain and rejection. You see, there is no such
thing as "painless love." The closer we come to somebody,

the greater potential there is for pain. We have all felt the pang of "let's just be friends."

As Gibran continues in The Prophet:

> "Like sheaves of corn he gathers you unto himself.
> He threshes you to make you naked.
> He sifts you to free you from your husks.
> He grinds you to whiteness.
> He kneads you until you are pliant;
> And then he assigns you to his sacred fire,
> that you may become sacred bread for God's
> sacred feast.
> All these things shall love do unto you that you may
> know the secrets of your heart, and in that knowledge
> become a fragment of Life's heart."

Ultimately we all have to make the choice of being a butterfly and risking the beauty of the unknown, or remaining in the safety of our cocoons.

Sometimes we seek safety because we are afraid of intimacy. For those of us who have lived four, five, six, or more decades, the temptation to protect our hearts is tremendous. But if we are happy within ourselves, and have triumphed over our negative self talk, we will probably dare to risk again and again. The pot of gold at the end of the rainbow is well worth the effort.

Thoughts To Silence Our Negative Self Talk

Know that everything passes.

Remember that you were able to overcome everything up to now. The proof is, you are alive.

Focus on the rebuilding, on the hope, on the possibilities.

Surround yourself ONLY with positive people.

Remind yourself that everyone has made mistakes, had difficult times, and that is the nature of life.

Laugh at your inner whining and don't let it spill over on your conversation.

Help others who are in a worse situation, and be grateful for what you have.

Understand that it's human to be depressed after a loss.

Give yourself time to grieve.

Realize that as it's OK to grieve, it's also OK to be happy again ... no matter how devastated you were.

Relinquish the temptation to judge yourself.

Accept what is, and let go of what could, should, might have been.

Acknowledge that you did a good job ... you didn't have to be perfect.

See setbacks and failures as strengths; opportunities to grow.

Stay in the moment, and forget about the end result.

Be open to being more and better when the worst has passed.

Give unconditional love to everyone, because the more you give away, the more you will get.

Let those whom you love into your life, and believe their positive descriptions of you.

Give yourself a hug, (if no one else is around to give it to you), and say "You Did a Good Job." And know that you did!

An Exercise To Exorcize Your Judgmental Mind

1. Close your eyes.

2. Relax. Hear your breath as you inhale and exhale. Concentrate on your breathing for five minutes.

3. In your mind's eye, write down the negative things you have called yourself.

4. Look at the words, and then tear the paper into a thousand pieces

5. Throw the shredded pieces of paper into a bonfire and bid them good-bye.

6. Watch how, little by little, the papers disintegrate, and how the wind blows them away forever.

7. Now, write positive words that are the opposite of what you first wrote.

8. With your eyes still closed, watch yourself as you press these new, empowering words to your heart.

9. Open your eyes. Write the loving words down on individual sticky Post Its, and repeat them as if you believed them.

10. Put these positive reminders everywhere in sight, and continue to say them out loud everyday until they are part of your belief system.

And, once you have conquered your negative self talk and fears, and opened to love and intimacy, one way you can maintain that love in your heart is by writing a Heart Sutra, which is the essence of Buddha's teachings on wisdom. The core of your Heart Sutra is gratefulness to the other person in your life. It is part of living in conscious joy and focusing on the positive.

Thich Nhat Hanh, the Buddhist monk and pacifist, tells us to go to a private place and write down, from our hearts, our own unique expression of gratitude towards our loved one, and then to put it in a sacred place and chant our Heart Sutra everyday. I was recently given a beautiful, Chinese silver container by someone very special, with the purpose of depositing my dreams, with the hope they would become realities. I have chosen to also use it as the sacred place for my Heart Sutra.

A Personal Story

You might have noticed I began writing the What and How of this book when I was 61, and I am now almost 63. And you might have been confused about the time frames. During the writing of "Jump and The Joy Will Follow", there was a six month delay in which my first editor kept blaming the computer for not transposing my words properly. There would be extra letters, or missed paragraphs, or spelling mistakes that had nothing to do with the chapters I sent her. My editor, feeling my frustration, assured me that this had never happened to her in twenty years of successful editing. She told me I wasn't going to like what she had to say, but I had to accept that the universe didn't want my book to come out. To say I didn't take her explanation with kindness is an understatement. Why wouldn't the universe want my words out there? It made no sense at all.

Today, however, it makes all the sense in the world. She was right. I truly believe the "forces to be" knew that something important was about to happen, but all of the stars weren't aligned yet. I also believe the universe (God, destiny, life) wanted me to be able to add this addition to the last chapter, as proof of the core of this book: if you jump, if you hold on to a dream, if you are prepared emotionally, physically and spiritually, the joy WILL follow.

The universe is calling me to take a gigantic jump I never contemplated or imagined. It is to a far away place: China. This sacred journey began with an exchange of e-mails with a man who lived in China and wrote in French. His name is Louis-Guy. Our only interest at the time was to exchange thoughts about the books we were writing. Never imagining we would meet, and without the need to impress, in our more than 300 letters, we both permitted ourselves to be completely honest and vulnerable. It was through the sharing of our inner reflections and our willingness to be transparent that we started to learn about each other, and discover we shared the same vision and dreams of life.

Since then, he traveled all the way from China (where he presently lives and teaches) to meet me for the first time in Puerto Morelos. There, in the place where I have found such happiness, our virtual connection was confirmed. So, it is I who am now preparing my trip to China to learn about his world. Our intention is to eventually work together as a team, to make this a fairer, safer, happier world. Sound familiar? Maybe, just maybe, my visualization has come true.

We know there are no certainties, and we are both cognizant that all poems don't rhyme, and all stories don't have a happy ending. However, we also agree the true reason for jumping is to open ourselves to the unknown, since life is about graciously and gratefully living the journey, not focusing on the ultimate destiny. It is precisely the not knowing, the ambiguity, along with the wondrous things we learn and experience on the road, that I believe is the essence of life and the message I have always conveyed to my daughters.

Hence, this book has ended, but a new chapter in my life is just beginning ...

Bibliography

American Heart Association. The American Heart Association's Low-Fat, Low Cholesterol Cookbook.

Andes, Karen. A Woman's Book of Strength, Penguin Putnam, 1995.

Berg, Karen. God Wears Lipstick, The Kabbalah Centre, 2005.

Blair, J.H. The Hot Spots, The Best Erotic Writing, Penguin Putnam, 2001.

Block, Joel D. Sex Over 50, Reward Books, 1999.

Bolen, Jean Shiboda. Older Goddesses in Everywoman, Harper Collins, 2001.

Bolen, Jean Shinboda. Goddesses In Everywoman, Harper and Row, 1971.

Brockway, Laurie Sue . How To Seduce A Man and Keep Him Seduced, Citadel Press, 1998.

Bortz, Walter M., II. We Love Too Short and Die Too Long. Bantam, 1992.

Brown, Helen Gurley. Sex and the Single Girl. Barricade Books, 2003.

Brown, Helen Gurley. The Late Show, Avon Books, 1993.

Butler, Robert. The New Love and Sex After 60, Ballantine Books, 1976.

Chodron, Pema. Good Medicine, Sounds True, 1999.

Clark, Etta. Growing Old Isn't For Sissies, Pomegranate Artbooks, 1995.

Conrad, Christine. A Woman's Guide to Natural Hormones, A Perigee Book, 2000.

Crenshaw, Teresa. The Alchemy of Love and Lust, G.P. Putnam's Sons

Dowling, Colette. The Cinderella Complex, Summit Books, May 1, 1981.

Dowling, Colette. Red Hot Mamas, Bantam Books. 1996.

Dyer, Wayne. There is a Spiritual Answer to Every Question, Harper paperbacks, Sept. 2003.

Garcia, Oz. The Healthy High Tech Body, Regan Books, 2001.

Grudemeyer, David and Rebecca. Sensible Self Help, Willingess Works Press, 1995.

Hafen, Brent Q. et al.   Mind Body Health, Simon and Shuster, 1996.

Keesling, Barbara. Bad Girl's Sex for Good Girls,   M.Evans and Company, 2001.

Keesling, Barbara. Talk Sexy To The One You Love,   Harper Perennial, 1996.

Khalsa, Dharma Singh. Brain Longevity, Warner Books, 1997.

Kravich, Sally Pansing. Vibrant Living, Spk., 2002.

Labowitz, Shoni. Miraculous Living, Simon and Shuster, 1996.

Love, Susan. Dr. Susan Love's Hormone Book, Random House, 1997.

Lynch, Jerry, Chungliang Al Huang and Al Chung-Liang Huang. Working Out Working Within, The Tao on Inner Fitness Through Sports, Putnam, 1998.

McArdle, William. Essentials of Exercise Physiology, Lippincott Williams and Wilkins, 2000.

Peal, Norman Vincent. The Power of Positive Thinking, Printice Hall Press, 1987.

Pogrebin, Letty Cottin. Getting Over Getting Older, Berkley Books, 1996.

Reinisch, June. The Kinsey Institute New Report on Sex, St. Martin's Press.1991.

Ruiz, Don Miguel. The Four Agreements, Amber-Allen Publishing, Nov. 1997.

Schwarzbein, Diana. The Schwarzbein Principle II, Health Communications, 2002.

Sheehy, Gail. The Silent Passage, Random House, 1991.

Smith, Kathy.Moving Through Menopause,Warner Books, 2002.

Snowdon, David. Aging With Grace, Bantam Books, 2001.

Somers, Suzanne. The Sexy Years, Random House, 2004.

Tenneson, Joyce. Wise Women, Bulfinch, April 2002.

Thich Nhat Hanh. Love In Action, Parallax Press, 1993.

Thich Nhat Hanh. Call Me By My True Name, Parallax Press, 1991.

Treguer, Jean-Paul. 50+ Marketing, Palgrave, 2002.

Valliant, George. Aging Well, Little Brown and Company, 2001.

Vliet, Elizabeth Lee. Screaming To Be Heard, M. Evans and Company, 1995.

Viorst, Judith. Forever Fifty,Simon and Schuster
Viorst, Judith. Suddenly Sixty, Simon and Schuster, 2000.
Viorst, Judith. I'm Too Young To Be Seventy, Simon and Schuster 2005.

Wolf, Sharyn. So You Want to Get Married? Plume Books, June 1999.

Yogananda, Paramahansa. In the Sanctuary of the Soul, A Guide to Effective Prayer. Self-Realization Fellowship

Magazines

The Oprah Magazine, Age Brilliantly, Oct. 2005.

The Art of Aging "Going Public" Vogue, Fall 2005.

Time Magazine, Feb. 2, 2004.

Breakthrough Digest, August 21, 2003.

My Gratitude

Words aren't enough to thank the following people who not only made this book possible, but contributed and supported my Jumping.

To Vivianne Oubiña, I send more love and appreciation than can be put on paper, for giving me her valuable and objective feedback, for her loving confrontation when my ideas lacked clarity and for being patient with my daily calls and e-mails. I am also indebted to her sister, Vannessa Baqueiro, for her uncompromising honesty which forced me to dig down deep and live up to her high standards. To Jenny Rodriguez, for giving me the encouragement to Jump high when others would have preferred my feet to have roots.

My heartfelt gratitude to Laura Baker for her wise suggestion I combine beauty secrets with love letters; to Rebecca Price for making me realize there is more to life than meets the eye; to my brilliant and "picky" editor, Bill Maule, who wouldn't let me get away with anything, although I tried; to Christian Riggs, who not only created the beautiful cover and layout, but is an example of a man who has achieved a loving and balanced life.

I want to also acknowledge Daniel Galindo, the talented photographer, who has immortalized all of our recent celebrations, and made me look like I could fly on the cover of the book. My thanks to Nora Jacobs, my eclectic friend from Puerto Morelos, who is also responsible for many of the beautiful pictures. To Eva Silva, my best friend, sister and guardian angel who was always by my side, words will never be enough to express my love and gratitude. I cannot leave out my friend Craig Collins whose walks on the beach brought me back to life, and Mitch and Lori Thrower for their unconditional help and literary suggestions.

The essence of this book and the ability to go into the unknown would not have been possible without my health. For this most valued of all gifts, I am eternally indebted to Dr. Michael Barnett for his integrity and intuitive healing; Doctors Kikawwa, Granet and Levi for giving me back my sight; Dr. Raul Lopez Infante for restoring my esthetic balance; and Dr. Diedre Elliot for going beyond the expected, and discovering my Graves Disease.

Most importantly, there is Toño and the entire Nacif family who never stopped reminding me the most important gift in life is family. Thank you. Wherever I go I take with me your heartfelt lessons and unconditional love that are reflected in my life and the letters I wrote to my daughters.

Finally, I send pride and gratefulness to my brother, Richard Berman. Our parents would be so happy to know it was thanks to him I learned to look inside, instead of the mirror, to find my worth.

And to Louis-Guy Reid for being the Joy that followed from my Jumping higher and further than I myself, thought I could.

The End.

Linda Nacif has a masters degree in clinical psychology. She is a professional bilingual speaker who has shared the secrets of how to create a masterpiece of every stage of life with audiences in Latin America, Europe, and the United States for over fifteen years. She welcomes your comments at www.lindanacif. com, where you can learn about her self-empowering retreats in Acapulco and her speaking engagements.